THE APPALACHIAN BIGFOOT

DR. RUSSELL JONES

BEYOND THE FRAY
Publishing

ISBN 13: 978-1-954528-19-2

Cover design: Disgruntled Dystopian Publications

Beyond The Fray Publishing, a division of Beyond The Fray, LLC, San Diego, CA
www.beyondthefraypublishing.com

BEYOND THE FRAY

Publishing

In memory of my grandfather, Thomas Brooks, the greatest outdoorsman I've ever met. He nourished and encouraged my understanding of all things outdoors. May the winds of heaven blow gently and carry the whisper of your dogs in the distance.

CONTENTS

FOREWORD

MATT MONEYMAKER & CLIFF BARACKMAN

The subject of Bigfoot field research (i.e. not just the collecting of newspaper articles) is roughly sixty years old now, in 2021. Roughly half of that period occurred prior to the Internet. Bigfoot field research in the Appalachian Mountain range did not begin in earnest until well after 2000. Only a few investigators like Sam Sherry went into the field prior to 2000 in Appalachia.

There have been a few conferences for Bigfoot field researchers in Pennsylvania over the past two decades, but it's a small scene compared to Ohio. There is a book with old newspaper clippings from Pennsylvania from the late 1800s and early 1900s describing encounters with these creatures, but nothing else in book form focusing on Pennsylvania Bigfoot research into the modern era.

The author of this book, Dr. Russ Jones, wrote the one and only book about Bigfoot research and sightings in West Virgina, so he is the obvious person to write the book about Bigfoot sightings and research for the whole Appalachian range. Russ has led Bigfoot field research efforts in Ohio and West Virginia, and he has been involved with the BFRO for many years. Consequently he carries most of the accumulated knowledge about how these creatures operate in general, and where these creature spotted in the Appalachia.

Russ urges me to write a book myself about Bigfoot field research, to document everything I've learned over the years. I've toyed with the idea, but I already post a lot on the BFRO web site so it always seemed redundant. However, when I read this book about Appalachian Bigfoots, I realized how much knowledge and insight (behavioral and geographical) has been gathered over the decades that I had forgotten or almost forgotten, much of which I taught Russ years ago. It all still holds true, and it is so good to see it in print, in book form. Be glad that you have a copy. The Bigfoots in Appalachia are not going away, and the information contained herein will not be obsolete any time soon.

- Matt Moneymaker

Over the course of my twenty-seven years of bigfoot research, I have had the opportunity to visit 46 states and five continents in pursuit of sasquatches. As one can imagine, I have met a huge number of people in these travels. Some of these people loudly proclaim them-selves to be bigfoot researchers, but few in my opinion have risen to this lofty claim. Dr. Russ Jones is one of these few.

I have always been struck with Russ' quiet demeanor, never making his research about himself, but always keeping his eyes on the prize: learning about sasquatches. The best woodsmen know that to be familiar with any animal, one needs to be knowledgeable about not only that animal, but all the others, and the environment in which they live. No animal, not even sasquatches, are isolated, but rather integral parts of a larger ecosystem. To these ends, Russ has furthered his own research by becoming a certified naturalist in his state.

When television productions, bigfoot researchers, or bigfoot enthusiasts go to West Virginia, Russ is always one of the first researchers to receive the call for help. Having worked as a BFRO investigator for many years, he knows more witnesses in his region of the country than anyone else. His knowledge of the habitat is intimate. His intelligence can be seen in his work, as well as his creativity in deploying novel techniques and experiments. He puts more time and effort into his studies than anyone else I am aware of in his part of the country.

I was honored to be asked to write the foreword for his first book back in 2015. Having been asked again does not lessen the honor, rather it amplifies it. Russ has become a good friend over the years and is one of my "inner circle" with whom I discuss my own research openly. I actively seek his advice and knowledge in my own work, and value what he shares.

Through this book, Russ is sharing his knowledge with you. It is a rare thing to sit at the feet of someone as experienced as Russ. Take what he says to heart and know, as I do, that you are hearing the thoughts and experiences of a lifelong investigator.

- Cliff Barackman
November 2021

PREFACE

I have been interested in Bigfoot since I was a young man and believe that I have had encounters with the creature. While not seeing the creature in the clear, prolonged way I desire, I have heard noises, sometimes even aggressive noises, found hair, and have found footprints. None of the animals of Appalachia are capable of producing what I have found. It gave me a hunger and thirst for Bigfoot knowledge when I finally came to believe what the answer was.

I have a bachelor's degree in science, my doctor's degree is in chiropractic. I am a certified master naturalist. So my background makes me come at things from a science perspective but with my consideration of a lifetime as an outdoorsman. I was fortunate to grow up in one of "those" families that hunted anything and everything from plants to animals.

My standard to believe is high. I know that this can frustrate some witnesses and other researchers. I just believe that people are biased in how they see things, wanting to see what they want in many cases. I also believe that if you are going to claim that a large primate exists that hasn't been "found" yet or a body procured, then it's a huge claim, and the evidence procured must be the same, and you should err on the side of caution.

Nonetheless, come with me on this journey. Come with an open mind and an honest cynicism. It's fine to question the concerns you have and share your doubts, you should, but it's intellectually dishonest to not consider all the evidence.

INTRODUCTION

Much of the Appalachian landscape resembles the Pacific Northwest: steep, remote mountains, and lush water-filled valleys. Of course, the Pacific Northwest is the most common region for Bigfoot sightings, so why would it surprise us that the region on the east coast most resembling it would be renowned historically for Bigfoot sightings? For the purposes of this book, I will be considering Appalachia to be how it was defined originally by the federal government in 1964 during the "war on poverty".

The War on Poverty was proposed by President Lyndon Johnson during the State of the Union in which the aim was to "not only relieve the symptoms of poverty, but to cure it, and above all, prevent it". It included Medicaid, Medicare, the Food Stamp Act, the Economic Opportunity Act, Job Corp, and Head Start. It included the following states: Pennsylvania, Maryland, Ohio, West Virginia, Kentucky, North Carolina, Tennessee, South Carolina, Alabama, and Georgia. Later, as more money became involved, more states were added, many not having anything to do with Appalachia.

In terms of Bigfoot, Appalachia, and this book, I will be choosing the five states with the greatest number of sightings in the region and therefore representative of the region. The more "traditional"

Appalachian states, if you will. It by no means implies that Bigfoot is not found in relatively large numbers outside the Appalachian foot-print on the east coast or in other parts of the states that a portion of which fall into the Appalachian footprint.

It will go something like this. I will visit many of the states to look around in person in the area that they have a lot of historical Bigfoot sightings. I will interview what I consider the best or most active Bigfoot researchers through Appalachia. I will try to give you a feel of what it's like to be in the woods in Appalachia or give you an idea of where to go.

The Appalachian Mountains themselves are roughly 1,500 miles long and 450 million years old. Though now averaging just 3,000 feet in height, the Appalachians were once as tall as the Rocky Mountains and the Alps. They are among the oldest mountains on planet Earth.

Also, for the purpose of this book, I'm assuming that Bigfoot exists. For much of my life I would have told you that I'm "95% sure" type of thing. I would have said, "Until I saw one dead on the ground, I won't be sure". I've moved past all that, and it only seems fair to be honest and clear about it. Somewhere along the thousands of inter-views and tens of thousands of hours in the woods, I became certain. More on that later...

1

BIGFOOT IN APPALACHIA – THE BEGINNING

I f there is anywhere in North America it exists outside of the Pacific Northwest, it's in Appalachia. Many of us believed for many years that it could only be in the Pacific Northwest. That area makes sense, of course, because whatever Bigfoot may be, it came across the Bering Strait ten thousand to twenty thousand years ago. Appalachia is a largely remote area where the morning fog eerily hangs in the hollows. Steep, forbidden mountainsides that in many places are inaccessible that just make you feel like Bigfoot belongs there.

Sure, there are large cities in Appalachia, think Asheville, Birmingham, Chattanooga, and Knoxville among others. Even within a half hour or so of the largest Appalachian cities you can be in a remote area that makes it hard to believe that a large city is anywhere near.

It's easy for people to believe or assume that Bigfoot is a myth. Never in our history have we as a society spent less time outdoors. We are largely afraid of the dark, getting lost, the animals out there, not to mention snakes. During many interviews or podcasts that I do, it's common for me to hear: "It seems like if something like that is out there, then someone would have found them by now." I always want to who "someone" is? There's no one out there. Of course, I have proof of this on all of my game cameras. Appalachia in places is very remote.

It's easy to see the resemblance between the pacific northwest and Appalachia.

I literally went years in West Virginia without seeing people on one of my game cameras with the exception of the cameras that I put out on trails and trailheads in order to get an idea of how many people were using a particular trail. In Ohio it's hard to find a place where at least a couple of times a year someone doesn't meander past. I remember one camera that I placed in West Virginia's New River Gorge. I had to drive to a remote dead-end road, hike a mile on a seldom used trail, then up a steep mountainside off trail that takes an hour to get a quarter mile. If I took you there, you wouldn't believe a person would ever be there. I was covering a "flat" on a mountainside with this particular camera. A "flat" being a flat part of a hill or mountainside. Sometimes there are several on the hill or mountainside before you reach the top of the hill or "ridge" as it may be called. I would move the camera along the flat, on top of the flat, on the bottom of the flat, with the sun, against the sun. I believed in the past that I had heard a Bigfoot sound in that area before, so I was trying anything to come up with a Bigfoot picture if one came through the area again. Well, you guessed it, after a year no Bigfoot pic, but I got one of an older gentleman staring at my camera! You go places deep and remote, and you should assume that others may as well.

The small percentage of our society that is actually out there seldom ventures farther than a quarter mile from a road or trail, and that's even been documented.

Myths seem to fit and be natural in Appalachia. Appalachia's population is largely stagnant in most areas. The residents are older than the average nationally. They are less educated and racially diverse than the general population in the rest of the country. Heck, if you visit our fairs, you will find that we even have "storytelling" competitions! For a city dweller who seldom ventures into the wilderness, a stereotype is formed, which in turn can make it easier to discard a subject out of hand. That Bigfoot doesn't exist in their city or environment but rather in an area they seldom go; maybe their perception of the people living there doesn't lend itself to serious consideration or even a conversation. Let's face it, people are busy with their lives, jobs, families, and who follows the happenings in Bigfoot world enough to be educated on it? Most would be surprised that there's people who actually do! In the end seeing (or sometimes hearing) is believing, and if you aren't there and if Bigfoot doesn't live where you do, then it's hard to imagine one existing.

Interestingly, nationally about a third of the residents of North America believe in Bigfoot. The thing about that is it includes Chicago, New York, Los Angeles, and all the other enormous cities where Bigfoot doesn't live near. In the Pacific Northwest or Appalachia the percentage believing in Bigfoot can be as high as 75%. Almost any hunter or outdoorsman in those regions has a strange story or a friend with one.

The author caught on one of his own game cameras on a remote mountaintop.

As I have mentioned before, I want to believe. Does that mean I can't be scientific and objective? No, of course not. It's a romantic notion to believe that there are things out there left to be discovered. I crave the lonely, isolated, and solitary places. What better thing is there than if a Bigfoot is there and to have the excuse to walk there looking for evidence and hoping against all odds for an encounter.

2

WHERE ARE THE BONES?

You can't talk about Bigfoot without figuring out how they get their food. An average-size adult Bigfoot is larger than an average-size adult male human and requires more calories. Also, the average human is much less active than a Bigfoot would be, spending much of the day hunting or scavenging for food. This is one of the first questions I considered when I became interested in Bigfoot. Is there enough food around to support this animal? A bear takes a lot of food but in some places may hibernate six months. Would looking at an orangutan or gorilla be commensurate in this aspect? I acknowledge that after looking at this issue, it's only a concern in colder weather areas.

Today, for instance, as I write this, it's in the 20s Fahrenheit. Snowing and a couple of inches on the ground already. Being an outdoorsman, I know that most of the game is "lying low" and not active until the storm is over. My guess here is that Bigfoot would as well. Staying in a cave, rock overhang, mine, abandoned structure, or pine groves. Although they (Bigfoot), like other predators, prefer the higher ground, they may stay lower during a storm. Here at my house in West Virginia the elevation is 1,600 feet. A five-minute car drive away the temperature will be warmer by several degrees and half the snow. Drive the other way forty-five minutes and its ten degrees cooler and twice the snow.

I suspect that food being the primary concern, it's a subject addressed for most of their lives. In most places where a Bigfoot may exist, water is not a concern except for extremely dry periods. Space without humans is primarily the next concern. They can't stay in one location unless there is a food source, as they would exhaust it. For instance, in Ohio there was a case of a Bigfoot family group that was staying in a wooded area of 1,200 acres surrounded by agriculture. They were in the area a few months, and several local individuals had had a sighting. By the end of their time, there was no roadkill in this location either, as they had exhausted food sources. It seems that they stayed in this location for an inordinate amount of time, and some speculated a baby Bigfoot or an elderly Bigfoot, but who's to say.

Since they have learned all the food sources to them in an available area, and we are assuming Bigfoot in this book, there is a comprehensive list in another section. Even there I'm sure I will be forgetting some.

Through Appalachia deer are overly abundant and can be found most anywhere. In some places of the country the deer aren't as populated, and asking, "Where are the deer?" as a postulate to finding a Bigfoot may be reasonable but not in Appalachia. Almost any field in Appalachia will have deer feeding in the evening. In fact, it would make me question what was in the area if I didn't see at least a couple of deer around. So, all this being said, I don't believe that the "circuit" is based on deer at all rather than other food sources and especially "treat" foods. I described treat foods in the *Tracking the Stone Man* book that I wrote a few years ago and believe we should consider it a reason for a Bigfoot being in an area of a sighting. In essence, a treat food is a food not found commonly; it's seasonal or annual. Examples would be berries, gardens, orchards, etc. It would be most commonly a sugar since that's so hard to find in abundance naturally in nature. It could be farmer Blevin's garden, an apple tree somewhere, a place where fishermen throw away fish parts, definitely not something available all the time. I believe they are conscious of treat foods in an area and always around for them. Then they opportunistically kill a deer, eat roadkill, or visit a dump. In Bossberg, Washington there were many sightings by the townspeople of a Bigfoot that was crippled and seen limping around the town dump. Tracks were cast, and these were paramount in convincing Dr. Grover Krantz that Bigfoot was in fact real. After reconstructing the anatomy of the broken foot on the cast, he believed it unlikely that someone without training in anatomy could have produced such an example.

Kleptoparasitism, according to Wikipedia, is a form of feeding in which one animal takes prey or other food that was caught, collected, or otherwise prepared by another animal (including humans), including stored food. Quite a few examples of this come to mind of this and may be the primary reason that someone believes they have a Bigfoot in an area without an actual sighting. Hunters all over the country talk about deer that they have shot or even already hung up disappearing. It's interesting to note that a few years ago scientists monitoring grizzly bears found them to be paralleling hunters, just out of sight. The bears had learned to wait for a hunter to kill an animal and then get there first to take it. Surely an animal more intelligent than a bear would learn to do the same thing.

In my book *Tracking the Stone Man* I wrote about perches. A term I coined concerning an area where a Bigfoot may safely watch humans or an area. It's always connected to an area of deeper woods and/or provides a route of escape. Most commonly a food site but may also be for protection. When I go to an area, say at park dumpsters (for an example of many), I get out and think about where I could sit in seclusion and watch the area. Usually, a couple of spots are apparent that you can go check out. If active, you can find tracks, broken sticks, and other signs that something has stood behind the brush, trees, or rocks. In the course of time, you can find them fairly often with experience. That's one of the first things that I check out in an area to see if it's active. So, in my mind it looks like this. Bigfoot stay farther back during the day in an area inhospitable or at a place where humans don't frequent. As darkness approaches, they move to the perch area and wait for humans to clear out. Once they do, they visit the dumpster, trash cans, dump, garden, orchard, etc.

Probably the most famous example in Bigfoot history of kleptoparasitism is the Ruby Creek incident, which happened in Canada in 1941. A woman and her three children were outside their remote cabin when they saw a seven-and-a-half-foot Bigfoot coming down the hill in back and fled to town. The husband and a deputy sheriff went to the location immediately and found seventeen-inch-long footprints going to the shed and dumping a barrel of fish out. Eventually it went back to the woods, stepping over a four-foot fence in the process.

A group of 19 trees and a twist found near a perch area.

Bigfoot is an omnivore, which means it feeds on both plant and animal matter. Bigfoot is an opportunistic feeder. They use their lifetime of knowledge of where food is at different times of the year. He will take food in the form of what's in dumpsters or roadkill. He will kill as he needs to get food.

Interestingly, I have seen several cases of what I believe to be a Bigfoot feeding on trash cans at shooting ranges. The ranges are usually located in remote locations, and humans aren't commonly in the woods around them. If you know of a shooting range in a park or large woods, it might be a good place for you to check out.

Have you heard that in Subway restaurants in Europe, they aren't allowed a tax exempt for their bread because it contains too much sugar? I think our food wastes found in trash cans and dumpsters full of fast-food bags are another source of sugar. They would be as addicting to a Bigfoot as they are to a human. In many places in parks where people go to shoot or hike, or even just sit, they leave their leftovers as a secondary food source.

3

MY FIRST BIGFOOT SIGHTING

I suspect that most people who got interested in Bigfoot had an experience and got interested, and that's me. If you have read my writings or followed my talks, you know the stories that got me interested. It's rare that I don't do something Bigfoot related at least at some point in the day, whether it's communication with a witness, writing, or looking at maps, or some days, like today, all three.

The last couple of years the amount of Bigfoot activity I have experienced has markedly increased. You see, I used to be anywhere within four to six hours of the house. Although I was out several days a week, I seldom made it to the same place more than a few times, well, because of time, although I spent so much time in the woods! I was up to thirty game cameras, thirty-two, and now thirty-six, and I have to get to each of them every now and then.

The reason that my Bigfoot activity increased is because I stopped spreading myself so thin. I concentrated my time on just a few areas and stuck to my Bigfoot calendar. If there was a Bigfoot sighting or encounter of some type by myself or others, I marked it on the calendar. I went to that location if it was around that time, or if nothing was marked, I would investigate a new area. I also moved a number of the cameras in the areas I was investigating. This has really helped me become more familiar with the area, its animals, and their patterns.

Previously I had found that I had experienced Bigfoot activity roughly every two hundred hours that I was in the woods. Not necessarily a sighting but sign or noises. Once again, always during the day. Now using my Bigfoot calendar, it's about every sixty to one hundred hours.

On this day I was walking in a park because during the same week two years prior, two gentlemen had a Class A sighting (clear visual) there. Of course, that's not a guarantee that a Bigfoot will be there again, but it's a shot. It had rained a lot the night before. When I got to the park where I was going in, there were no cars, and it would be around a four-mile hike for someone to be around.

As I started on the trail, I noticed that in the mud there had been no one else there. As I started climbing the hills, I could hear kayakers on the lake laughing and thought how curious that must make any Bigfoot around, and they might want to take a peek. Shade, my faithful lab, was off leash and about twenty feet in front of me like normal. Movement at my one o'clock caused me to glance over, and what I "saw" was a hiker sixty yards from me in some brush that was buff colored all the way up and had a backpack. Thinking I would be meeting a hiker, I whistled to Shade and put his leash on. The leashing took no more than ten-seconds, tops, and I walked on. Quickly the trail turned to the left, and I realized that what I had seen was off trail. Suspicious immediately, I ran to the spot and then a close ridge just twenty yards farther, where I could see the whole area in all directions. No hiker, nothing, I would have seen one. Now looking at the area, I noticed that whatever it was came down the hillside through the thickest area available and was in a pawpaw patch when I saw it. This group of trees was five to six feet tall. What I saw was about a foot to a foot and a half taller. It's interesting that our brain attempts to categorize what we see instantly into something it knows or is most likely.

I was talking to esteemed Bigfoot researcher Matt Pruitt about the brain categorizing sightings of different things, not even necessarily Bigfoot related. He told me that many times in the infamous "Area X", the members of the North American Wood Ape Conservancy have seen something walking upright and instantly assumed a team member was walking there even though they knew that none were in the area. Once again, the brain categorizes it as something that happens more often and reliably, maybe what would be expected in a situation.

The author on a typical day carrying cameras into the woods.

So, you can imagine that my "sighting" is not the one that I desire. I already have it pictured! Me, walking up a holler, I make a bend in the valley, and there he is walking sixty yards away, walking right to left. Well, maybe it will happen. Since that experience I have started wearing a GoPro many times when I'm in the woods. Even if I just got another one-second glimpse, I would have enough for everyone to look at.

4

A NORMAL DAY IN THE WOODS

So, what is a normal day like in the woods for me? Some of it I have covered, but in an effort to be complete, please bear with me. For some, maybe many, you don't have a great deal of choices. Maybe there isn't that much woodland around you. Maybe you are driving to a state park or national land because that's close to you. When I first got started, I would be anywhere within a five-hour radius and have hiked all state and national land in that radius. I kept looking for the elusive virgin Bigfoot that hadn't seen many people up close and was going to come right in and give me some form of evidence. Trust me when I say that it hasn't happened that way yet. They are generally curious about humans yet reticent in their behavior much of the time. I suspect they are present around us more often than we think they are.

As much as I like going to new places, as time has gone on, I have concentrated my Bigfoot efforts into areas that I believe are active and are reasonably accessible to me so that I can get there throughout different times of the year. There's one large park that I frequent that is spread out over dozens of miles wide on a straight line. I hiked about two hundred hours before I even heard or saw anything that I thought was Bigfoot related although I knew they were in the general area. That should give you an idea that it's not easy to come across a Bigfoot.

It's all about data, and at present we don't have enough to reasonably predict where on a given day we could expect a Bigfoot. You can collect reports from groups, your own, or both. Go into those areas and hike on and off trail. Put your cameras out, throw some gewgaws (trinkets) on a log or in a cave, and see what happens. Put some peanut butter, Nutella, bits of honey, or sweet mix. Eventually with patience and time, maybe patterns may begin to emerge for you.

There is a report in a general area that you know of each August. You found track in December. Once again with every piece of evidence asking "why would a Bigfoot be in this location?" It's not by chance; it's either food, security, or on the way to another location.

Remember that we are talking about a very large animal, so food is always a consideration. Sugar and carbohydrates can be hard to come by naturally in nature. Are there certain times of the year that you have berries? Of course, there can be large patches anywhere, but concentrate on right-of-ways or clear-cuts that are remote with no four-wheeler access but in an area that has a history of Bigfoot sightings.

The three most common places for a sighting are a road sighting, a hunter, or someone in the woods; it's something to keep in mind. Driving is, well, driving.

When we are in the woods, we can act a lot like a hunter, as they have a lot of sightings. Wear camo, move slowly, sit still for long periods of time. It's a tactic to try. You may try to just act like a hiker or camper and be cognizant of the sounds around you. Many do that with great success. Probably many hikers have Bigfoot activity around them but aren't familiar with the sights and sounds of Bigfoot, and it goes unnoticed or passed off as being something else.

Shade, exhausted after one of our long hikes. In warm weather we try to stay near some form of water.

When I go into the woods, where I go is based on data that I have for that time. I know where I have heard them in February, July, and September. I know of other months there has been suspect activity on game cameras in March and October. I know of other months where there are sightings at a certain general place and location each year. This is how I decide where I place most game cameras and where I am going to hike. I am going in the daytime where I can not only hope to see them but find evidence of them or their passing. From November to April when there aren't leaves or briars, I am off trail all the time. If I have a time that I don't have anything on my "activity" calendar, then I use it as a time to be in the woods exploring a new place that I have noticed on maps. I have dozens of places awaiting me now that are new that I want to explore. Always expanding my knowledge and walking in different parts of each area. Of course, a camera slung over my shoulder and another in my pack.

I think that it's important to find an organization to your exploration. When I go to a new area the first time, I will walk all trails if there are any there. The next time I may walk all the creeks. The third time I will walk all the ridges. After several times I will feel that I have a grasp of the area.

5

CITIZEN SCIENCE

I don't know of any university paying for or participating in Bigfoot research. I don't know of the government giving anyone grants to do Bigfoot research. I've said for many years that Bigfoot research will be done by the Bigfoot enthusiasts, and then when definitive proof is obtained, the university professors and researchers will come out from behind their desks and take over.

To the professors and the researchers, a bunch of people sitting around a campfire cooking bacon doesn't look much like research. Now you and I know that we can't sneak up on a Bigfoot. It's a good idea in an active area to hope to pique interest in an animal that's curious about humans and likes to sneak food from humans when they can.

One day Bigfooter and television star Cliff Barrackman and I were talking to a famous primatologist trying to get game camera pictures of a known species. They were using hundreds of cameras in a straight line so many feet apart, even if a camera was right up against a tree. A couple of years later and still no pictures, that's the reality of science. She was curious about where Bigfoot camera traps were being placed. The answer was something like ridges, flats, funnels, bottoms, and saddles. She then said, "Well, how do you know that they travel in those areas?" Science establishes where they travel. We must continually try new ideas and then with success be able to reproduce them, establishing a hypothesis.

Bigfoot mockup as created by artist and investigator Bo Bruns.
This is the same model that Cliff Barackman has in his museum.

The reality is that while the scientist would stay in place for weeks or even years, getting paid to do it, the Bigfoot enthusiast has gone home after the weekend because they have to go back to work the next day.

What would it look like if actual scientists were doing Bigfoot research? Well, first of all the people doing the research would have degrees and be trained in scientific methods. They would be in the very best locations. Some of the places that they wouldn't let you and me go such as watersheds. They would be there for great lengths of time. They would have the newest and best "toys". Remember that they won't be out there until there is definitive proof.

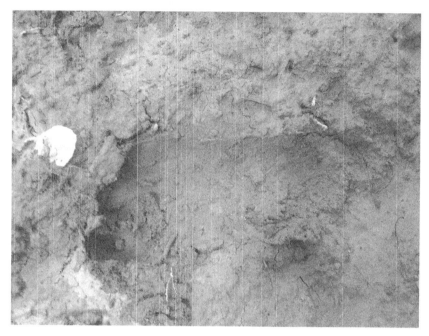

A possible 16 inch Bigfoot track. Like Chimpanzees and mountain lions, I believe Bigfoot to be cognizant of the danger of leaving prints.

Notice how some of the things the enthusiast does is the same as the scientist? While we don't have the time, or necessarily the toys, there are things that we need to do better than we do. I've written about documentation. I'm going to the woods today, and as soon as I come out, I will sit down and write my thoughts. We need to find time to be in the woods more. Choose a location or locations that can be accessed more often and frequently. The mystery won't be solved by us sitting in front of our computers and going to the woods a few or several weekends a year. Try to evolve your techniques or ideas. That's certainly one thing the internet is good for. Openly share ideas and findings. My experience is the east coast researchers, the Bigfoot stepchildren, share freely most of the time. The original children, the west coast researchers, can be protective and don't like to share as freely. I get not wanting to give specific locations, but findings and ideas are something different.

One thing that I regretted in the past was taking the *Finding Bigfoot* television show to active Bigfoot locations where I had success with what I believe were Bigfoot interactions. The public shows up after the episode in your area airs, and many times it's never the same. Recently I participated in a special episode and gave up a special location with activity. I guess I figured I had been there a lot of years and only came up with a couple of casts, so what was the harm? Maybe some new people will come with different ideas than mine and come up with some good evidence. It would drive me crazy if they just walked around screaming and banging sticks against trees.

6

DOCUMENT YOUR TIME IN THE WOODS

One of the things that I have realized in the years that I have been researching Bigfoot is the importance of documenting my time in the field. Of course, I had always kept some notes, but after a conversation with a fellow researcher, I recognized my need to step it up. Now as soon as I come in from the woods, I sit down and write my thoughts about that day in the woods. I include where I was, which is boxed in, so I can easily go back and find other times that I may have been in that particular place. We should always be trying to add to our data. The goal is in the end to come up with when is a Bigfoot going to be in a certain location and at a certain time. Another reason that I always keep a game camera up for at least four seasons in each location and also hike each location in each season.

Once again, due to caloric requirements, it is not likely a Bigfoot, or a family group of Bigfoot, would stay continually in one location unless the food supply can support them. Don't forget that aside from the carrying capacity of that particular area of woods, it's possible that a habituator could be helping supply food. Saying that reminds me of a case in a tract of woods surrounded by cornfields. Five separate farmers had had sightings of different members of a Bigfoot family. They apparently didn't stay in the area year-round, but interviews had shown that at some points there were absolutely no road-kill in the area.

A location that the author believes he has had several Bigfoot encounters.

I also record the time, temperature, and weather conditions. Generally, I will go out in the woods regardless of the weather except maybe during cold rain in the winter. I figure that Bigfoot is out there somewhere, so I'm not going to get any evidence sitting on the couch. It seems like a good reminder, if you have heard me speak, that I now almost exclusively go in the woods during the day. Very little evidence is collected at night save some thermal footage that doesn't seem to be compelling to anyone but the Bigfoot community. I believe night-time bigfooting is primarily for experiences and not evidence. It's a blast to do with friends and is important for newbies (first-time Bigfoot expedition participants) to have the experience.

I also mark rock overhangs, mines, game cameras, doodads (trinkets), Nutella, peanut butter, or whatever else I have in the woods. When I got to thirty game cameras, I was able to still remember somehow where they all were even without notes or GPS pins. Admittedly, different times of the year can make me have to look around for a few minutes sometimes! I think I must have to thank my grandfather for my ability to largely not get lost in the woods and remember my way to different sites. He took me for years to remote hidden spots, many times at night, sometimes without a light to sit and wait for a dog while he would check on another. I was certain I was going to be eaten alive at any time if not for the grace of God having some plan for my life! In the 1970s we didn't have all the great headlamps and flashlights that we do now. Heck, we didn't even have warm boots that were waterproof. Grandpa walked with a carbide light that was essentially a bright candle while brushing branches that would whip my cold face as I followed along blindly behind him.

I also keep track of my general thoughts of the woods that day. Was there a place I should have left a camera? Did I hear or see something? Did I see other animals? What kind of tracks did I notice? What was the majority of the type of trees? Was there year-round water in the area? It could be different for me than others. In West Virginia and Ohio there are a lot of places that I go where I seldom see anyone, and the game cameras prove that seldom is anyone around much of the year in some places.

A ground blind or nest type structure. Note the many twisted branches used.

Proper and thorough documentation is probably the one area sorely missing, aside from time in the Bigfoot woods, by those in this pursuit. The reality is that many in the Bigfoot world don't care about documentation, scientific methods, or keeping records. They enjoy the socialization and fellowship, not to mention the stress release of the time in the woods. All of that is fine, and I enjoy it myself, it's just not research.

7

COLOR IN THE BIGFOOT WOODS

I'm sure you must wonder why in the world there would be a section in a Bigfoot book on color in the woods! Some people believe through gifting or just things that they have found in the woods that Bigfoot may be able to see certain colors or may be interested in certain colors. Of course, we don't know for certain, and it would depend on where and what lineage Bigfoot may be to gather the information except anecdotally. For instance, some feel as though Bigfoot may be related to an orangutan. They are solitary creatures, as Bigfoot appears to be, are relatively large in size, and have reddish-brown hair that many supposed Bigfoot hairs appear to be under a microscope. Some feel that lemurs are the magic species, others somewhere in the homo line, and on it goes.

One thing we can say for certain is that Bigfoot comes from the "Old World primates". Old World primates are those primates that originated in Africa and/or Asia. The reader may remember that the population that fills North America came from Africa and/or Asia ten thousand to twenty thousand years ago via the Bering Strait.

I commonly leave toys, colored rocks, etc. in remote locations as curiosity lures.

Old World primates see trichromatically and have excellent binocular vision. Trichromatic meaning seeing red, green, blue and the hues in between. This may aid in detecting ripe fruits and vegetables, even in treetops. It also aids in seeing movement, which is important for seeing prey or avoiding other animals or humans.

New World primates, coming from the Americas, are not generally confused with a Bigfoot. They are mainly smaller monkeys. Their eyesight is very variable to excellent trichromatically, and they have excellent binocular vision.

Another point to consider is that animals with the best eyesight are diurnal, meaning they are active during the day. Some have speculated that Bigfoot is lemur related, but that seems unlikely because prosimians, such as lemurs, have poor color vision. They have dichromatic vision, which means they can differentiate greens and blues but not reds.

So now that we understand what type of vision that it seems Bigfoot is most likely to have, back to colors in the environment and if they may mean anything to them. Like humans, it stands to reason that a color different than the surrounding environment would stand out. For instance, the woods are green or dark most of the year. A brighter color like blue, red, or yellow would stand out in that environment. If you look at the internet, many of the "experts" will tell you that Bigfoot is very interested in the color blue. Maybe he is, but maybe it's because it stands out?

There is a Bigfoot researcher in Kentucky who puts peanut butter out in the woods, duct-taped to trees. He told me that Bigfoot will only mess with it if it has a red or a yellow lid. Fortunately, Dollar General stores sell peanut butter with red lids for a dollar, so give it a shot. Currently I probably have forty to fifty jars of the red-lidded peanut butter scattered over a couple of states. So far, I have had two interesting incidents. In Ohio's second most remote location, I had a game camera that was locked disappear two years prior. I had no idea if someone or something had taken the game camera. Almost two years later I had a peanut butter jar disappear three-quarters of a mile away from the game camera location. Three months after that, the lid of the peanut butter showed up against the base of the game camera tree! It made me feel that when in a good location, possibly they are around more than we realize. My close friend and investigator Brad Kennan told me that they may have been communicating that they liked my peanut butter but not my game camera!

In another remote section of Ohio woodland, I had a jar of peanut butter out three miles off trail show up a couple of miles from its location when my good friend Dr. Kenny Brown was hiking. Imagine my surprise when I received a text with a picture asking if "this was one of my peanut butter jars"!

The lid from the type of peanut butter I use with a primate pheromone chip on top.

My suggestion would be that if you are interested in possibly attracting a Bigfoot, whether possible or not, consider the color of the environment and use something contrasting. Of course, keep in mind that humans may notice too. I've had several interested people look at peanut butter jars taped to trees in the woods that I happen to have a game camera pointed at!

8

BIRD LANGUAGE

I mean, here you are in a Bigfoot book, and the author sticks in a section on birds? Well, if we remember, the most common way to have a Bigfoot sighting is from the road in a car. Dr. Grover Krantz, a legend in the Bigfoot world and the first academic or scientist involved in Bigfoot research, used to cruise the back roads of the Pacific Northwest with a camera and a rifle. He received an inordinate amount of grief professionally, and I'm sure that he did want to shoot one to prove that he was right. Many of my friends on the east coast have cameras mounted in their vehicle, just hoping for a lucky encounter, and I'm sure that many of my friends out west do the same.

The second most common way to have an encounter is to be a hunter. So, hunters do one of two things, creep slowly through the woods or sit stationary and quietly in the woods. Because you are in the woods, you always have a chance for a Bigfoot sighting, but I believe you have a better chance if you are sitting along the way. This is where birds come into play.

Nature has tattletales in the woods. The creatures of the woods work in concert against you, the interloper, in their domain. If you have been in the woods, you have heard the chipmunks screech the announcement of us approaching their territories. Birds even more so of a problem. In most of Appalachia in warm weather there are over a hundred types of birds present. In the winter there are around a couple of dozen.

A beaver dam is a smorgasbord of food for all animals.

It's interesting that when I take people in the woods, we've heard the bird sounds so much that we don't notice until someone points it out and we actively listen. Most birds have a territory about the size of a football field, fewer yet the size of a couple of football fields, and so on. From the time you get out of your vehicle, the birds are "alarming". Just walk into your yard and listen to the peeps. That's how we have gotten to the point we don't notice it; it's all around us when we go outside.

Birders and ornithologists (scientists who study birds) have learned that alarm calls can go from one hillside to another at 100 mph. There are certain calls across species that tell what type of predator is present, so to speak. Smaller birds worry about smaller predators because those are the ones agile enough to keep up with them. Larger birds are louder and more worried about larger predators. "Mobbing" is when a group of birds is carrying on because a predator is close by. By paying attention, you can tell which way the predator is moving and, in some cases, even what type of predator is present.

Sometimes it's smaller birds chasing larger ones; surely, you've seen this. The smaller bird, being more agile, sometimes chases the larger bird away from a nest or a food source. These behaviors give male birds a chance to show off their physical qualities and how good a mate they may be. Not surprisingly, crows are the biggest fan of mobbing, and we've all heard them carry on in the woods! Like nagging, this can go on for hours!

So football field by football field and moving across the hillsides at 100 mph, birds are announcing you coming through the woods and which direction you are going. If you decide to sit down for a little while, the birds will decide you aren't that big a threat where you are and settle down. One of the most interesting things about bird behavior, or "language" in this case, is that we are finding that mammals are learning to listen to bird behavior and even certain specific species of birds. Deer, coyotes, and bobcats will listen for the alarm calls. Even the direction in which the birds fly will show the animals which way to flee from the threat.

So an animal will set up downwind of where danger most often comes from and in an area where they will have a little view, then use the birds to give them an even greater advantage. Many times, the animal can escape even without being seen. Maybe you can understand now how unlikely it is to even run into a Bigfoot, even setting aside how rare they must be. We are likely to get a lucky sighting if Bigfoot is moving, staying near food, or has young or old in the area.

Woodsmen have been conscious of bird language in all likelihood going back forever, but our knowledge is expanding. There isn't evidence that Bigfoot is using this to their advantage, but I feel confident that if other mammals are aware of it, then we should take it into consideration.

9

HOW PEOPLE AFFECT YOUR RESEARCH

This area of the book came to mind because I lost three of my expensive Reconyx game cameras last week that had been chained to a tree. A park ranger had suggested an area that was remote and not many people go to. I had been there many times snooping around and heard what I believed to be Bigfoot there from February to early March. In anticipation, I moved seven cameras in an area that was pretty small, hoping to get lucky. This person messed up a lot of the work I had been doing. Even though it's a great area, I ended up having to pull my cameras out. There's a saying that "locks just protect you from an honest man". Well, mine were locked, but it looks like it's apparently possible to break them with a multi-tool.

A thief is just one way that people can affect your research. Too many people, the less likely you are to see a Bigfoot in most cases. So you have to find an area that is close enough to get to frequently but not with so many people to impede activity. If these animals exist, and they do, they have to have a remote sanctuary so to speak.

Once again, prior to the *Finding Bigfoot* television show, the public generally didn't know that there were sounds associated with Bigfoot. Shortly before that, "pre-internet", there was a very limited knowledge of anything Bigfoot. Now, it's not easy in some states to find an area that hasn't had the experience of humans yelling, screaming, and knocking on things. You just can't get much reliable research out of areas like that. There are Bigfooters in Salt Fork State Park in Ohio each day year-round. There are still sightings each year, but any Bigfoot activity there must be heavily vetted. During the first season of *Finding Bigfoot* when filming at Salt Fork, they sent three of us to the edges of the park to make sure no one was in the park or interfering with the show. Many of the reports in that area that come to the BFRO aren't investigated unless they are really special reports, because of the suspectness of a heavily researched area. So that means we have to find a promising area of state or federal land that isn't heavily visited or an area of private land that must be substantial. Preserves many times limit access, permit trail hiking only, and close at night. Another option is a property like my farm that adjoins a park.

Recently I took a report from a bright and well-spoken witness who had a sighting the week before. She and her husband have twenty-four acres adjoining just such a preserve. Her property didn't need to be huge, as the preserve limits access. Her husband mows trails for her to walk her dogs each day, which she does at the same time. She commonly sees deer, rabbits, and other wildlife. She had told her husband about a month prior to the sighting that "all the animals had disappeared". One day she got a late start walking, which seldom ever happens, and when she got close to the preserve, she heard a noise. She looked up to see, closely, only fifty yards away in a clearing, a gray Bigfoot. Its eyes appeared light, and its elbow bent like it may have been carrying something, maybe a young one? It looked at her and walked into the preserve.

Glyphs found in remote regions are not proof of anything but are intriguing.

I believe it or they had been around for the last month, and that's why she hadn't see the normal wildlife. I also think that it's likely she ran into the Bigfoot because she broke her normal pattern of behavior, walking later than normal. About a week later, all her normal animals were back. The preserve is probably not large enough for security or food long term, but a stopover in their circuit.

A woman, a witness, who never previously gave a thought to Bigfoot, is now consumed with it like so many thousands of witnesses. She knows that in the spring or the same time next year, she may again notice the normal animals hiding and keep her eyes open.

Large twists, the size of a wrist or larger is compelling but even more so with other evidence found nearby.

It's always a hard decision on whether to let people know the specific area where you do your research. I know one time I was in charge of a public BFRO expedition and opted to choose a state park that was Bigfoot active but not one where I spent the majority of my time. Once you introduce people to an area, they will continue to go back and will share with a few people. Another time I took a BFRO group to a West Virginia state park, and years later people in that group still go back.

Here's an example of the decision that you have to make. There's a gentleman well known in the scent industry. He sold scents and owned a company that is well recognized. He is also really interested in Bigfoot. Matt Moneymaker, of *Finding Bigfoot* and head of the BFRO, sent him to me. He developed a scent based on curiosity and another one based on primate sexual scents and pheromones. I chose a park in Ohio to try it in. He stayed in the location three days, loading the scent in two different places. I kept a camera on each, and a long duration recorder was put out. We worked it for months, and I kept the cameras out for over a year. Nada, nothing happened. There are so few of them maybe I didn't get close enough. Maybe the scent didn't interest them. Maybe they didn't come by then. Maybe they heard or smelled my game cameras, who knows. In my mind smell may not be their most developed sense. They have hooded noses, which wouldn't allow getting the most scent in the nostrils. I smell things in the woods, and there are reports of Bigfoot seeming to smell or "wind" (being downwind or getting a smell of something, often a predator) humans, so why not give it a shot?

Now the gentleman has a different delivery system and new scents that he wants to try. Do you let him into one of your personal areas or choose a different area? It's all about data, and you have accumulated enough that you believe that they are in a certain area a couple of months out of the year. You might get lucky, but you could push them out or make them more reclusive. It's not like you can get out in the woods as much as you desire as it is, but what if you mess up your area?

10

LET'S TALK ABOUT GAME CAMERAS

I f you are new to Bigfoot research, it seems like one of the most logical things is to put out some game cameras and get a picture of Bigfoot if he really exists, right? Would it be surprising for you to know that some people believe that Bigfoot hears, sees, senses, and/or smells game cameras?

I spoke at the huge 2019 Ohio Bigfoot Conference on the subject of game cameras, as I felt as though there was a lot of misinformation about them and strategies to deploy them in the field. In general people had some of the following beliefs. Bigfoot can see in the infrared spectrum, so therefore can see the cameras' flash. They can see the cameras because they know the woods so well "it's like their backyard". They see you put the cameras up, so they know where they are. In response, now that knowledge is coming along, we have to explain how modern game cameras work.

Game cameras themselves are fairly uncomplicated machines. They don't have a "beam" of light sticking out that Bigfoot can see even if they can see in the infrared spectrum. What they do have is a lens called a Frenzel lens. It has facets like you might imagine on a diamond. The system has a PIR sensor. The camera, when deployed and turned on, is sitting there passively monitoring all the infrared heat coming into it from the objects in front of the camera. If the sensor measures a difference in the heat, the camera fires.

Bears toy with game cameras many times because the plastics contain formaldehyde which can mimic the smell of anthills.

The price of game cameras varies wildly from $50 to $600. The quality of the lens, pixels, and electronics accounts for the difference in quality and price. Higher-end game cameras also have a "blackout" option, which is essentially a filter that blocks visible light coming from the game camera so that the animals or even humans can't see it (theoretically). The cameras aren't seen or located as easily, and many believe don't spook animals as much.

One thing we know now for sure due to studies is that animals can hear game cameras. They can be up to 30 decibels, and generally the cheaper ones are the loudest. Noise is essentially a product of wasted energy, so the louder ones will not have as long a battery life in the woods.

As far as smell goes, there is certainly an amount of time for new cameras to "off gas". The plastic chemical smell can last for months. Interestingly, that's one of the reasons that bears mess with game cameras. Formaldehyde, in many plastics, may smell similar to anthills. I couldn't tell you the number of times that a bear has messed with one of my game cameras. One of the worst things that happens is when a bear finds a camera shortly after it is put out and knocks it out of balance. One of the things in Bigfoot research that you can't replace is lost time. When you consider that some of the game cameras I put out I may not revisit for a year, it's a big deal.

As for seeing the cameras, it's true that many people literally stick a camera on a stick or a tree right in the wide open, and it's obvious. The lens can be reflective or even look like an eye to an animal in the woods, it has been reported. Any serious researcher worth his salt will make an effort to hide or disguise the camera. If you get the camera up out of sight or at a ninety-degree angle to where one expects the travel of most animals to be looking, it can help. Other tactics may include putting a camera under a log, cutting a piece of log or tree out in the shape of the camera and inserting it and covering it with the bark of the tree. You can put a ghillie suit on your camera, as they actually sell them! I gave them a shot, but rain and snow kept pushing the material down and interfering with the camera shots and function. I'm more inclined to believe hidden and out of the line of sight is best, but many times the very best place to

put a camera has no place to set one up! I carry the camera back out
of the woods more times than I actually put one out.

Be careful when placing winter cameras. This growth popped up right in front of
a possible Bigfoot track causing the author to miss a possible game camera shot.

In regards to seeing the infrared flash, I'm inclined to believe that it can be seen by a Bigfoot. It's really not an issue unless you are setting up in an area with a lot of traffic like a deer trail. I've found during my time in the woods that a Bigfoot won't walk directly on a deer trail but rather off to the side of it. When looking for an area, choose one where a Bigfoot may be but not every bird or deer, which will make you go through thousands of pictures and diminish battery life. That also helps prevent a Bigfoot possibly seeing a flash and a ruined setup. The Reconyx cameras I use (thirty-six at present) can easily last over a year in these conditions with lithium batteries. Many times, they will have over three thousand pictures on the SD card. I don't want to see three thousand deer and squirrel pictures.

In terms of Bigfoot seeing you put a camera up, is that possible? Sure, it's possible, but the reality is that Bigfoot are rare, and they can't be everywhere, so in all likelihood they aren't going to see you put every camera out. I think the most likely explanation of game cameras failing to get results is, firstly, how rare Bigfoot are and the small odds of getting one within fifty feet of your camera. Secondly, I believe that in all probability most animals, including Bigfoot, "hear" the cameras, for the reason mentioned previously.

Now that we believe we know what one of the reasons may be, electronic noise, we just have to compensate for that. As if it's not hard enough to find the right tree or setup, we also need something to help mask the noise! I am now using things like creeks, rivers, and roads, among other things.

One of the mistakes I feel that are made regarding game cameras is thinking it's all about getting a Bigfoot picture. Is a Bigfoot picture what I want? Sure! Would people believe and be convinced by my picture? Doubtful. Nonetheless, it would be another piece of evidence to add to the pile.

Other uses of game cameras that come to mind, assuming that Bigfoot can hear them, is to use it to your advantage. Block certain areas or attempt to shape their movement toward a better camera trap. Maybe move them toward an area where you want to sit. Another game camera finding that I consider is the wildlife that I see on them. For instance, if I have a camera in a place for a while and I see an average of twenty deer a day, and then all of a sudden for a period of time all the deer are gone, we should be suspicious. Could it be human, mountain lion, or Bigfoot movement that is affecting the animals? Sure, it could be anything, but it's worth keeping in mind. Habituations, or people who think that they may have a Bigfoot around their house, can put up a cheap game camera to help find out. If it's a coon, coyote, possum, etc., then the activity will continue, and you will see what it is, except studies show it's hard to get an alpha male coyote on a game camera. If activity stops while the cheap camera is out and then resumes when you take the camera away, it would make it seem that Bigfoot activity is a possibility.

We have to continue to hope that the technology will improve at the same time we work to think out of the box. Scientists with hundreds of game cameras and a staff struggle many times to get pictures of known species. Sometimes it can take years for them to get a picture. Remember, for all we know, Bigfoot may travel in some weird way we haven't considered. I suspect that once we figure out how Bigfoot travels, a lot of pictures will come out. Our efforts need to be consistent, calculated, measured, and lastly monitored. It's a massive task and undertaking to get a Bigfoot picture.

So how many game cameras are out there? How many game cameras do we need to adequately see what is out there? Well, of course, Bigfoot, like all animals, doesn't stay just in their "living room". I've discussed ranges in general because different areas of the country have different terrain, food sources, isolation, and of course number of Bigfoot. Also ranges in general because we just don't know. Assuming, and that's a big if, the cameras go undetected, I would like to have one game camera per twenty acres of woodland. We don't need cameras in cities or fields for a Bigfoot survey, so that cuts down on the area and therefore the number of game cameras needed. Choosing Ohio, because of the high number of sightings, the total number of acres of woodlands is around eight million. Interestingly, that has doubled since 1942. About 31% of the state is forested. If we use a game camera every twenty acres, we would need 400,000 game cameras to cover the state IF strategically placed. About 36% of hunters use game cameras. In Ohio there are around 426,000 hunters, which is down about a third since the same 1942 period. So, on average there are about 153,000 game cameras being used in Ohio. Clearly not enough cameras are in use to do the job. Additionally, they aren't being used strategically with each other, probably not being used year-round, many not hidden well, and most target deer.

Some states are in better shape. West Virginia has twelve million acres of forest land, so we will need 600,000 cameras. There are 350,000 hunters, so once again the number of game cameras can't cover the necessary woodland. Also, like many other states in Appalachia, in places there are many miles between roads and trails, sometimes dozens of miles. Not that Bigfoot may only be in remote areas, but it's unlikely that many of the game cameras get put in the most remote areas in great numbers. Hunters simply like to be able to get to their hunting location and don't want to drag a deer for a long distance. I just pulled a camera out with over seven months on it. 99% of all people on it were back after just forty-five minutes in the woods. They had to pass the camera on the way in and out. I do this setup in many cases to get an idea of how far back in the woods I have to get to go farther than everyone else most of the time.

Clearly by now you can see that it's hard to have enough game cameras in a strategic pattern. Add to this the cameras can't be seen, heard, or smelled, to locate an animal that is rare and probably in most cases may exist within only one family group per county, roughly. In 2019, there was a study to see how bonobos, chimps, orangutans, and gorillas react to game cameras. I should note that the game cameras didn't appear to be well hidden, but one thing that was noted, all the primates saw the cameras. They reacted in different ways, fear, curiosity, aloof, but they all noticed.

Much of the topography of Appalachia is so steep in places it's hard to imagine.

Of course, we have to hope that dishonest humans don't find our cameras. People always ask if I have lost any. Over the last decade I have lost four cameras. After finding Bigfoot activity in a specific woods, I moved seven cameras there and lost three in four months, probably to the same person. Generally, my cameras are so far into the woods that I don't see people on them. I kept hoping for a virgin Bigfoot, which would walk nonchalantly in front of one, but it has yet to happen. As my strategy changed to concentrate cameras in an active area that is smaller, it also made it more likely to encounter humans. A certain percentage of those humans are dishonest. At one point I went about three years without seeing a single person on a couple of dozen cameras. That being said, when I go into a new area, I may put a camera on the access point just to get an idea of how many people are using the area.

I like headwaters and places of consistent water supply as locations to snoop around.

I lock all the cameras up with a cable lock. A suggestion here is that if you are going to have very many cameras, get as many as you can keyed alike. Amazon offers about four cable locks in a group that are alike. When you get a bunch of cameras, it's a hassle to go through a lot of keys on a large key ring, and yes, you can lose them in your gear. I recently had a camera lock pulled off with what looked like a multi-tool. I think the old adage that "locks just protect you from honest people" may be correct.

In conclusion, here I am ten years later still trying new game camera strategies. Is it physically impossible to get a game camera Bigfoot picture for the reasons I cited? I still believe that it's a numbers game, not enough cameras hidden and strategically placed to get a picture of a rare primate. I have always used Reconyx game cameras, which are some of the most expensive. Recently they changed the design on the camera where the cable lock goes through, making it a hassle for people like me with a lot of game cameras. Maybe something cheaper or a different name brand will have different dynamics. I am in the process of trying out a few different brands now. In my gut I believe that I have had my cameras close to a Bigfoot and believe it's a matter of technique before a clear picture is retrieved. Once we figure out how to do it, I think that many of us will be able to succeed.

11

THE PROBLEM OF FIGURING PATTERNS

In this book I have talked about my "maybe" sighting. I was in the woods there and then because someone had had a Bigfoot sighting, and it was on my Bigfoot calendar. I felt more confident later about my sighting because the week after mine, two deputy sheriffs had a sighting of what they thought was a juvenile Bigfoot. It made me feel like the Bigfoot were in the park at that time, but are they always or just then each year?

A few weeks later I was in the woods with Dr. Kenny Brown looking around. We found a perch, remember what I said a perch is? An area set back from a popular area or food site where a Bigfoot stays, waiting for darkness or isolation before going into an area. It is connected to a larger wooded area for escape and security. The perch we found had seventeen twisted-off trees. It was another indicator of fairly recent Bigfoot activity.

So, now onto patterns. We need data to establish them, and the more data, the more valid and specific we can be. My Bigfoot calendar is not full of where there has been Bigfoot activity each week, all year long. Patterns need to be established and followed to be accurate. For instance, this year we had a late freeze in much of Appalachia. This in turn caused largely a wild berry failure and fruit trees not to produce in many areas. There was an increase in Bigfoot sightings this year; was it because the Bigfoot were more active in search of food following the late freeze? Because of COVID, the parks were packed all year like never before, providing more possible witnesses for sightings, and more food in the trash cans. So it's marked on the calendar; like other things it's "possible" data. Next year around the same time I will be there with my GoPro on, looking for sign. If there is valid data or even if it does not happen, I can sit down and get a better idea of why.

A 14-inch possible Bigfoot track cast by naturalist Joe Perdue.

In this field of largely citizen scientists, it is a reminder that much data may be "known" or "suspected" but not written down. Writing it down will jog the memory and automatically call for more information. We need to prepare for any evidence like a track or hair and know what we will do when we find it.

Recently I was going through my Bigfoot-related emails and saw correspondence with an older gentleman around eighty years of age. He used to spend time researching Bigfoot in one of the parks that I frequent. I touched base with him, and he no longer does anything Bigfoot related. He sent via email a map showing pictures and video of all the tracks and hair he had found and where it had happened. He had saved data, and I was able to add it to mine. Bigfoot world for each area is like a jigsaw puzzle, with you adding pieces if you notice or take the time.

Dr. Jeff Meldrum encouraged the author to write his first book.

Having knowledgeable friends, such as Cliff Barackman a must. Its important that they will tell you if the don't agree with you.

Having bright and trusted friends to go into the woods with a couple times a year is invaluable, Frank Ferguson and Brad Kennan.

Make sure you have friends that commonly may have varying viewpoints, Thom Powell.

The author with his grandfather whom he spent many days and nights in the woods with.

The author with friends Dr. Esteban Sarmiento and Dr. David Floyd.

*The author always enjoys getting to spend time with his friend
Bobo.*

*The author and Dr. Kenny Brown checking out remote rock
overhangs.*

Matt Moneymaker, of the BFRO and Finding Bigfoot, was instrumental in helping the author with a platform in Bigfoot research.

Matt Moneymaker with Shade. If you see Shade then the author isn't far away.

The author heard wood knocks from the top of this cliff face on two different occasions. It's a steep hour walk to get to the cliff.

Tunnels under highways are known to be a common location for Bigfoot sightings.

Old growth forests can be a sign that the environment and/or ecosystem has been similar for a long period.

The author's father encouraged his love and discovery of all things outdoors.

The author with the crew of the hit television show Finding Bigfoot.

The author with possible Bigfoot casts.

The author at a speaking engagement with Cliff Barackman and Dr. Jeff Meldrum.

A variety of trees and plants are a harbinger of a healthy environment.

I found this tree break after hearing it being broke and hearing a possible Bigfoot vocalization.

Possible Bigfoot knuckle prints found after finding a possible Bigfoot footprint.

Possible Bigfoot tracks in the snow. These are confused by galloping animals or hopping hares in many cases.

I find many places, primarily during the winter where bark has been peeled away in large sections. It's not something done commonly by known animals in Appalachia.

Rock overhangs can provide shelter, are a place for animals to get minerals, and a great place to look for tracks.

Vernal pools are an overlooked source of food and possible Bigfoot activity in the spring.

Finding these in the woods remind me of hidey holes my grandfather and I would set up for rabbits. Is it possible that a primate other than humans are smart enough to use them?

It's rare in Appalachia to find more than one Bigfoot track. If one steps on a path or trail the next step is usually in leaf litter and not discernible enough to cast.

An example of what Gigantopithecus may look like. Whatever Bigfoot may be in all likelihood came from Asia or Africa.

A possible Bigfoot summer bed, large, donut shaped, deeply impressed, north facing, stacked walnuts found on the edge.

12

TREE STRUCTURES

When I wrote my first book, I had a section on tree structures, but this topic has become so popular I decided to revisit it. We have people who are researchers who walk in the woods just looking for these structures. We've even had books written solely on the subject.

There are leaners, tie downs, Xs, and dozens of other names attached to them. There are internet groups just founded to post pictures of these trees. They also look at twists and breaks, which personally to me are more compelling. Of course, the honest answer is that no one can say completely, so it must be addressed thoughtfully and rationally

If Bigfoot exists, then he/she is a primate in a broad sense. They are hominoids, maybe the great ape family. The term relict hominoid has become popular, or hominin, which is closer to humans. Essentially all these words just mean in evolution or development. There are groups of species in the world that have remnant populations yet to be found. Bigfoot may be an example. On the other hand, Bigfoot could be *Gigantopithecus* or *Paranthropus*, something that has already been named. As time goes on, we are finding that there are many branches on the hominid tree, more than was originally thought. It has been discovered that these branches intermingle. For example, an ancient human (*Homo*) breeding with a Neanderthal.

While some structures can be interesting, I believe the great majority to be "forest litter."

So historically do hominids make tree structures? They do, with humans being the most developed. Even the most primitive hominids or great apes do as well. I believe it is much less common than what Bigfoot researchers believe it is to be. I don't think that Bigfoot or its juvenile get up and want to make vine circles like humans want to be on PlayStation.

Previously I have called all the debris found around the woods "tree litter". Joe Beelart, author of *The Oregon Bigfoot Highway*, says that "one in a million tree distortions may mean something". Now this does not mean that I don't pay attention, as it would be unscientific not to consider all the hypotheses. The term "perch" which I coined in my *Tracking the Stone Man* book, can be associated with tree distortions or breaks. A perch is a location a Bigfoot goes to observe humans or to wait for them to leave an area where there may be food. Think trash cans, dumpsters, fish remains, etc.

An example, Dr. Kenny Brown and I were in a park, looking around. There had been a possible sighting by me and another by two law enforcement officers. We found a location "perch" where it looked like something had been standing back from a lake trail that would lead to trash cans and such. Almost two dozen trees were snapped (couldn't have been done by a person, as two strong guys tried) from finger to wrist in size. Just a hundred or so feet away, closer to the lake trail, a twist was found. What makes this so compelling is that a hypothesis (perch) had been postulated, and the evidence was there to support it. That's not the same as just finding some random things in the woods you don't believe could have been caused by natural events.

Many of these "structures" are in pine forests or involve pine trees, which are notorious for having little root structure, and trees almost dance when falling down. People interested in structures should learn the tree types and keep notes about the common types involved. I carry a small field microscope to look at breaks, and many trees that to the eye appear healthy are actually diseased.

I believe that Bigfoot manipulate trees, but that it's not common. What I consider my strongest thought on the matter is our pioneers. Our forefathers were successful and knowledgeable woodsmen and hunters. They were in the woods each day and in many cases lived there. If these structures were as prominent as many would have us to believe, Bigfoot would have been discovered long ago! The pioneers and Indians knew the way of the woods and all the forest animals, and there's no evidence this was a conversation. The Indians talk about all kinds of Bigfoot-related lore, whistling, near water, walking ridges, taking women and/or children, not to be disturbed, etc., but they don't talk about tree manipulation. Evidence must be evaluated without an objective.

Sticks larger than your wrist driven into the ground with no dead trees nearby are curious.

13

HAVE YOU HEARD OF EDNA?

So have you heard of eDNA? Until around twenty years ago, no one else had either. In the last ten years it's become much more common. In the Bigfoot world there's much hope that this technology may be the test that finally helps prove the existence of Bigfoot.

Essentially what happens is as an animal, creature, let's say organism moves through an area to eat or bed, whether it's terrestrial (land), water, snow, or is in a cave, creek, permafrost, it loses DNA material. This DNA material is in the form of hair, skin, mucus, carcass, feces, etc. So if you happen to see a Bigfoot in an area, or want to see what is in a body of water, you take a sample and use a DNA sequencing method called either Meta barcoding or metagenomics. It's more successful if testing for a specific organism or animal, as you can amplify the test to take a closer look. As you look at it broadly, it loses some of its specificity and therefore effectiveness.

The advantage of eDNA testing is that you don't have the expense of putting a scientist in the field or the time involved for that matter. You could also go back to the same area and compare over the course of the years. eDNA is also used to help catch invasive species in different areas being tested, think snakehead fish or pythons.

Here's an example of the wide variety of things being tested: tracking earthworm communities, how long horse and mammoth survived in Alaska, pollen sediments to see which plants lived in a certain area, to find out if giant salamanders or tailed frogs exist in a Colorado stream, to find out if hellbenders exist in certain eastern US streams, distribution of invasive fish in a pond.

The Cranberry Wilderness Area in West Virginia is the largest Wilderness Area in Appalachia.

So, you can see it has a wide variety of applications, and the use of eDNA is spreading. Of course, certain scientific equipment is required, making it not a process that anyone can do, and of course there is a cost involved. Probably the largest problem with eDNA testing is contamination of the sample. From contamination when collecting the sample, in the lab, or where amplification occurs leading to magnifying of the DNA. This has caused some scientists to be leery of the testing. Nonetheless, if you came up with results showing the existence of a relict hominid, it should be fairly easy to reproduce even at different labs.

In the Bigfoot field there have been nests found recently in the Pacific Northwest, and eDNA is being attempted. One word of caution here, the sample degrades within forty-eight hours! So if you see a Bigfoot standing someplace, you can't just go collect the soil for testing in the future. That being said, you should of course go and look for evidence like tracks, hair, etc. and save it in a paper bag. At this point it seems like eDNA is excellent for subjects with a known genome but not as helpful for undiscovered species. Who knows what type of testing may become available in the future to test our saved samples?

14

LONG DURATION RECORDING

One of the relatively new forms of evidence is long duration recording. In the "old days" when we went into the woods, we carried a little hand recorder, and if we were really high tech, we would even attach a microphone onto our hat bill! As with so many things, technology is evolving, and the prices are coming down. In my estimation, about 10% of the Bigfoot researchers are doing long-term recording research.

How it works goes something like this. It's hard to find a recorder that can be set to control the time of recording. Most Bigfoot audio guys to present have been using something like an Olympus-DM 630, which now can really only be found on eBay. They construct a chamber using a four-inch PVC pipe about a foot long. One end is sealed with a hook, which can be hung from a tree. The other end is screwed end and gives access at the recording unit. The Olympus unit has a micro SD card. The battery on the unit is bypassed to be powered by D cell batteries. We stuff everything into the PVC pipe, and with some luck, you can record for about four weeks, more or less, if you choose to record from 9 p.m. to 6 a.m.

*A possible 14 inch Bigfoot track. 14 inches is about the average
Bigfoot track found.*

As I mentioned, I was a complete novice, so my friends Dusty and
Wes Ruth, father and son researchers out of Ohio, set up a couple of
units for me and instructed me on how to use them. I've also bought
a Song Meter and AudioMoth, which are new and coming from the
academic community. Using these last two, they have discovered
some new bird species around the world. They record for a couple of
weeks, have software analyze the bird sounds, and if something is
new, they send in field biologists. It's saving a lot of time and money.
Of note, you need to find a way to protect a recorder that has a microphone built in from the rain. Unfortunately many don't allow for
recording long periods of time.

The latest toy I am using is called the Swift, a terrestrial autonomous recording unit. It was developed by Cornell University Lab of Ornithology. Like so many other devices, this one is intended for birds, and Bigfooters, ever adapting, are using it. Powered by three D batteries, it lasts about three weeks and records on an SD card. Like the AudioMoth, they have been deployed on each continent. Since it's from a university, you lease instead of buying. You fill out an application, and on approval, it's $260.

A new device in 2020 is the Song Meter Mini from Wildlife Acoustics. At around $500, it's a small device that you change the settings via Bluetooth. If you are in a remote area, that's something that you need to consider. It records 240 hours on its AA batteries, so if you record 9 hours a night, you will get close to a month's worth of recording. A couple of cool things about this are that you can get lithium batteries and record for almost two years. Software is sold with this and, though expensive, will identify all birds for people interested in that. In my mind, developing information about Bigfoot is all about collecting mass data. Utilizing these long-term recorders is a way not only to know the noises a Bigfoot may make but also where they are at different times of the year. This in turn allows a chance to capture more evidence. Personal experience shows that for whatever reasons Bigfoot don't seem to feel as threatened by audio recorders as they do game cameras. Many times they will approach audio recorders and seemingly play with them and even sniff them. Sometimes they will even move them. This technique seems as though possibly the best unobtrusive way to monitor their location and movement.

One time I was with a group of friends for a weekend of bigfooting in a remote location in the mountains of West Virginia. One of my friends had an LDR that we placed a mile or so off trail for the weekend. On leaving Sunday, I walked in to get it with him. To our surprise it wasn't where we put it; it had been moved a hundred yards away!

A couple of problems with the audio recorders though. It seems as though there are constantly bugs in getting it to function correctly.

Any time that happens, it's lost time and data that you can't try to replicate for an entire year. Battery life is an issue. You don't want to have to walk into a remote location every week or month, especially if you are running multiple recorders. It looks like in time that the change to lithium will resolve the issue. Of course, a big problem is that the best setups are expensive. Hopefully, like everything else with technology, the prices will continue to drop. If someone wants the ability to participate in Bigfoot research without going deep in the woods or even going very often, then this is an option to do it. Of course, the largest problem may be the time that it takes to review all the recordings that you accumulate. Using software, like renowned Bigfoot audio experts David Ellis and Monongahela do, makes it quicker going in many circumstances, providing that the recording is in a quiet, and I mean quiet, location. I set up a recorder near my farm to see if there was activity near it. The closest neighbor is a half mile away, and the farm borders a park for three-quarters of a mile, and it was shocking the amount of noise picked up in a quiet location. You have to take a lot of time to go through the recording, and it's a challenge in today's lifestyles to spend so much time doing that.

15

HABITUATION

This is a word that is common to Bigfooters, but probably no one in the general public would have an idea of what the word means. To me, a habituator is someone who is either knowingly or unknowingly feeding a Bigfoot or affecting the behavior of one. The easiest examples are like this but not limited to it: A lady likes to feed wildlife and throws her dinner scraps outside each night. Old man Jones doesn't allow anyone on his property and really enforces it. Jim saw a Bigfoot one time and puts things out to see if anything messes with it. Things like toys, marbles, or other trinkets. Bigfoot Investigator Kennan leaves food and glyphs out in different locations and continually checks to see if he can get a Bigfoot interested if one is in the area.

I've worked with quite a few habituators over the years aside from trying to be one myself. Some of not only the best evidence, but also the best stories come from these people. It may well be from a habituator that the irrefutable Bigfoot evidence comes from.

Possible Bigfoot handprints left on a vehicle. Prints have a waxy type of sebum substance on them. The substance has been termed Sasquatch Alba Vernix by investigator Shelly Covington Montana. It's postulated by Monsterquest famed Doug Hajicek that it may be a way to acquire DNA.

One sweet woman from Central West Virginia was deer hunting when she saw something digging in the ground. It wasn't huge, but seeing a lot of bears, she knew it wasn't one of them. She was only fifty yards from it. She kept watching, and eventually it turned and looked at her before running away. She talked to me, and we talked about how to set up a feeding station. Something was taking the food, and although we were careful about how we set it up, anything could be taking the food. So I do what I commonly do and suggested to her to get a game camera. Not a nice or expensive one but the cheapest one she could find. If you're a feeding a raccoon, possum, or other critter, you will get a picture of it and know. If the feeding stops when the game camera is put up, but starts again when it's taken down, you may be onto something! When she put up the cheap camera, something threw sticks at it until the battery died. She is still feeding as far as I know. She tells me they seldom take all the food and prefer yellow apples to red.

Another habituator I talk to exchanges gifts and trinkets. She says they will sometimes come during the day if no one is at home.

Some habituators have a sighting, even enough times to name a Bigfoot "Fred", but in the course of time get scared of the interaction and break off any attempt to communicate.

I have talked to dozens and dozens of these types of people and probably a couple of dozen who are afraid and just want to know how to keep them away. The answer to that is motion lights and dusk-to-dawn lights.

As I've mentioned, and will again because it's interesting, the struggle with many habituation witnesses is that many times they stop worrying about getting evidence and place more value on the relationship with the creature. They can tell story after story but have collected little or no evidence. Another common issue with habituators, and with witnesses in general, is that everything becomes a Bigfoot or Bigfoot related.

It's important to remember that these are large animals requiring large amounts of calories. If they can't get enough food, they move along, generally following a general path established through the generations. In the majority of the cases, they pass through in the same season or seasons.

16

GIFTING

To some it may seem weird to have a "gifting" section in a Bigfoot book? Ten or fifteen years ago, no one would have been talking much about gifting. It's not something a new witness would be talking about generally, but more of a long-time witness type of thing. Several hundred witnesses later, it's a thing. Here are a couple of examples from witnesses. I have created pseudonyms for the witnesses in order to protect their identity.

Jill had a Bigfoot sighting near her home, and it made her wonder if they were around her. She found a place high up on a stand in the woods that other animals and birds couldn't get to and began leaving fruit, vegetables, and other treats. With some success some of her items disappeared. Her grandchildren, knowing that she loved yellow flowers, brought her a bouquet of yellow flowers that she left on her back deck. The next day when she went for her morning walk, she found her yellow bouquet of flowers up the mountainside in the middle of the trail. Jill was curious but took the flowers back home. The next day on her walk there was a group of all yellow wildflowers that had been picked lying in the trail in the same location.

*Food, toys, and colorful objects can all be used to tempt a
primates curiosity.*

Jane was called by her husband because when he went into the
woods to cut firewood, he saw a large pile of berry limbs that had
been stacked up. He believed that he had interfered with something.
He found it curious but her more so. She didn't previous have an
interest or belief about Bigfoot but couldn't imagine what in nature
would stack limbs of berry bushes. There was a prominent log in the
area, and she began to leave things on it, placed prominently, like
treats and toys. When something began to take them, she added a
shell from a beach trip that had both halves connected so she could
open and close it and put things inside. She would put things like

small treats or toys inside and in turn would receive things like a feather or rocks in place of her item.

As time went on, sometimes it would happen and sometimes not. Jane had eventually left a ball, and it showed up on her deck. Now that it seemed that whatever was interacting with her knew where she lived, it set off interactions that have went on for years and still today. Living in the country, they leave their garage open. Every now and then a rusty tool shows up in the middle of the garage floor, apparently taken at some point and out in the weather enough to rust and then brought back (maybe something playing with it?). Glyphs left on the deck are rearranged, and toys are taken and brought back.

Melody had seen a Bigfoot on two occasions when she contacted me. I suggested leaving curious things (a bell, toys, etc.) out near the house but out of sight. One night deep into the night, Melody heard something bang into the side of the house. On going outside, she found a limb up against the house at a place where no trees are. When going back inside, she noticed a bell that she had placed in her Bigfoot gifting area sitting in the rocking chair she always sits in on the front porch. It frightened Melody, and she quit trying for interaction. I haven't heard from her since.

Interaction is a good word in these cases, as that's what people are hoping to do. They believe that they may have a Bigfoot in the area, and they want to interact with it. My experience is that sometimes the Bigfoot will interact, and other times they won't. My hunch is that juvenile Bigfoot may interact more than adults, or the Bigfoot are staying in one area for longer than usual for whatever reason.

At my house I have deer in my yard all day long. When my dog Shade and I moved in, they would run or be on alert. After a few months they would stand and eat very close to us, paying little attention to us. They had become familiar and used to us. One of the things that I have tried to do is to use familiarity. Instead of being all over a couple of states each week hiking, I concentrate on a few different parks. I'm trying to breed familiarity with the animals there if it's possible. I may even pause at the same location and eat, leaving a little food behind. I'm hoping, if possible, to have something think "there's that guy who likes to walk in remote areas where we don't see many people, with his dog that stays close to him and doesn't chase animals".

Most habituators who try to interact value the relationship they believe they are having with a Bigfoot and worry little about the actual evidence collecting. Many, many things will take food or toys left out. Squirrels, humans, raccoons, ravens, etc. commonly do take things, so an honest effort must be made to rule that out. Maybe put out a cheap game camera that is loud and obvious. If the action stops, then returns when the game camera is taken away, then maybe you are onto something. I also try leaving cameras out with no batteries in them, trying to familiarize animals to seeing one, and then later I will add batteries when they no longer pay attention to the camera.

I see no harm in leaving different things in the woods, hoping for some action. I commonly leave peanut butter and Nutella duct-taped to trees in remote areas. Sometimes a game camera is watching over it and other times not. At worst if we ever have to bug out, I have stockpiles of peanut butter stored in the woods! I commonly leave colored rocks, marbles, small toys in areas like remote rock caves, stumps, etc.

I had three colored rocks on a stump with a game camera carefully hidden and guarding them, and the camera and rocks all disappeared even though it was two miles off trail. At my farm in Ohio, I leave sealed containers of sweet mix out but no cameras watching. Sweet mix is a grain mixed with molasses sold at feed stores for cows and horses. There are historical accounts of Bigfoot liking it. I have had one container disappear so far. Do I know that it's a Bigfoot? No, but no harm in dabbling with it.

A bigfoot in Appalachia, as described by witness, art by investigator Sybilla Irwin.

It's one of my core beliefs in Bigfoot research to always be changing and evolving, trying new methods and techniques. Who knows, maybe Bigfoot can't resist green plums, and that's the secret to attracting one in! It's a challenge for a solo researcher, so it's important to have friends that you can bounce things off of. My friend and researcher Matt Pruitt is one of those guys for me. Matt is involved with the North American Wood Ape Conservancy, which is a group of bright and like-minded individuals always pushing the envelope. Although I'm a long time BFRO member, I'm largely alone in the woods all the time without a second opinion or idea readily available.

17

BAD WEATHER

Yesterday I was in Columbus, Ohio, and was driving back to southeastern Ohio. I got caught in a snowstorm. The day started off 50 degrees and rainy, and by the next morning, it was 16 degrees with eight inches of snow on the ground. I wonder if there was anyone like me driving in the mess, wondering where the Bigfoot population was huddled down. When I'm in the public, aside from "Where are the bones?" "Why not more game camera pictures?" and "Why isn't there a body?" the next thing that people are curious about is where does Bigfoot go in bad weather.

The easy answer is the same place as all the other animals. Most animals aren't in holes or caves but rather just finding the best spot that they can. It could be that they just don't look at the cold weather like we do. I remember a report in the high mountains of West Virginia where a hunter was out on New Year's Day, and the temperature was in the single digits. In this particular area a creature the size of a Bigfoot could have walked to a much lower elevation in a couple of hours that would have been 10 to 15 degrees warmer. Instead, here it was doing what Bigfoot do in a much cooler place.

Deer, coyotes, bobcats, etc. the normal animals in Appalachia curl up in thick areas and out of the wind. There's no evidence of

Bigfoot using caves, abandoned structures, or mines for long-term use, but I would suspect that maybe they do to weather a storm. I have been in abandoned structures, and they are scattered throughout Appalachia. Concerning coal mines in just West Virginia, it's estimated that around ten thousand of them are abandoned and may have access. There are caves available throughout Appalachia, as well as rock overhangs.

A couple thousand feet in elevation can make a huge difference in temperature and conditions.

I remember one winter I was out following coyote tracks in the snow and came upon an opening just a few feet high under a rock. When I looked in, I could see train tracks and several small handcars. In the old days without heavy equipment to close mines, they just shoveled the opening closed, if they bothered at all. Over the years the dirt settles, and I can assure you that animals in the area know these openings.

Pine groves provide great protection and can be 10 to 15 degrees warmer than the surrounding area during cold weather. I spend a lot of time looking for remote pine groves in the winter for that reason. There have been some nests found throughout the country, and while it's much warmer than being up off the ground, they don't look to be built with warmth in mind.

Bears, like Bigfoot are omnivores and found in similar areas and habitats. They are in all likelihood responsible for many of the misidentifications.

I've spent many, many days looking for Bigfoot tracks in the snow and have not found any. It's led me to believe a couple of things. If they move around much when the snow is on the ground, they must be in deep remote places that are not commonly explored at that time of the year, or they are in pine forest types of places that don't leave tracks.

It's common to get pictures sent to me during the winter of "supposed" Bigfoot tracks. Some of the tracks look legitimate but most are cascading or galloping animals like rabbits, coyotes, or dogs. People look at the large track hole and distance between the prints and assume Bigfoot, as it's hard to think of any other animal that's tracks would be so far apart. With dry snow it's almost impossible to tell what made the tracks. It's helpful to take pictures close and directly down into the hole of the track. Many times, the sun, even in cold weather, will begin to melt the track and make it appear larger. By all means, don't forget that Bigfoot come in all sizes, and so do their tracks. The smallest track I've seen is four and a half inches, and the largest was nineteen inches. Fourteen inches is about average.

Going back to caves and structures, I believe evidence, or more evidence, would be found if it happened regularly. I remember Matt Moneymaker, of the BFRO and *Finding Bigfoot* television show, telling me of a cave in the Southwestern US that he found curious. It was found high on a cliffside with a view of the valley below. It was layered with a large bed of grasses that were intricately woven. I, once again, suspect that Bigfoot may use the caves, structures, etc. for limited use during inclement weather. Of course, I may be led to believe that because of the steaming fresh tracks that I found as a young man coming out of a cave following a snowstorm. That's before I even knew of such a thing as Bigfoot. What I wouldn't do to find tracks like that again!

Food, security, and safety must be at the forefront for an animal like Bigfoot if they are to exist. Since they were young, they would have learned where the food and cover are year-round, not to mention every little hidey-hole that is around that humans don't go near.

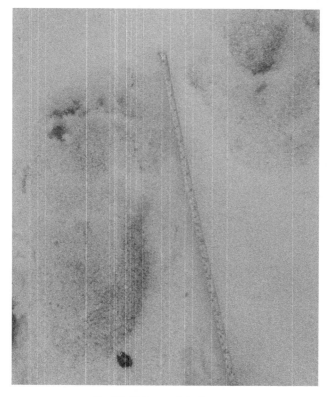

Possible Bigfoot track in the snow.

Of course, the best way to survive is to not expend as many calories. There are some recent 2020 findings that humans hibernated in the past in order to survive winter. Maybe a form of torpor similar to what bears do may be an option for Bigfoot survival. In the far north, bears may hibernate as much as six months. In the southern US where it's not as cold, bears may go in and out of hibernation, and this is called torpor. The more food that is available to a bear may determine the amount of time that they hibernate. This may be a consideration for Bigfoot researchers.

18

FOODS IN APPALACHIA

I remember one time walking with one of the master naturalist instructors and being told that in a typical healthy Appalachian forest, there are over a hundred things to eat. Probably for most of us the things in the woods, aside from animals, don't sound very appetizing.

Maybe some of the population might recognize some raspberries or blackberries, but mostly we would be afraid to eat anything.

Ever watch a deer walking through the woods? It nibbles on this plant, this bud, another plant, and so on. Inherently and through learned behavior, it learns what is edible. Many times, such as winter I'm sure, it's not the most desired food, like plump honeysuckle or clover, but rather just anything that won't make it sick. Bigfoot is an omnivore, a crea-

Many foods, such as these chicken of the woods, reproduce in the same areas year after year.

ture that eats foods that come from both plants and animals. They are opportunistic feeders, and I've covered ways that they get food. Below is a list of plants, fruits, nuts, and mushrooms commonly found in the woods and are edible.

In much of Appalachia when the foliage is on its hard to see farther than 20-25 yards and seldom any cell signal.

I was helped with the list by my friends amateur herpetologist and master naturalist, Jon Tinney and Joe Perdue. It's full, but I'm sure not comprehensive. I'm sure that many times we are walking through the woods and pass by evidence of feeding without even being aware of it. I remember one time seeing a stack of sumac saplings lying in a stack along a path. They weren't large, maybe the size of a large finger. I tried pulling some out of the ground like these were. There was no way beyond some giant man they were coming out, but here lay several beside each other. They clearly hadn't been dug up. I had another witness find berry limbs stacked that had berries on them. The nests out west were made of huckleberry limbs, presumably picked when full of berries. It's hard for us to think of food in terms of something completely different than we do. It's another reason for us to be in the woods more than we are and in all seasons. In terms of most plants and fungi, December may be the hardest month to find edibles.

Use caution with fungi and mushroom and be able to identify the edible ones. They can provide a year-round food source.

Mushrooms (requiring little to no treatment to be safe)

Morels
Omnipresent *Laccaria*
Chicken of the woods

Hen of the woods
Shrimp of the woods
Hedgehog mushroom
Black trumpet chanterelles
Smooth chanterelles
Golden chanterelles
Hollow-stem larch *Suillus*
Inky caps
Short-stem *Russula*
Tent stakes (yes, a plant, not literally, lol)
Aspen bolete
Bicolor bolete
Birch bolete
White pines bolete
The king bolete
Old man of the woods—must be peeled
Slippery Jack—edible once the cap is peeled
Birch polypore—edible when young
Honey mushroom
Bear's tooth
Lion's mane
Coral fungus
Crown coral fungus
Grey oyster
Pearl oyster
Winter oyster

Plants

Common nettle
Dandelion
Death nettle
Chickweed
Ramps

Wild onions
Honeysuckle
Clover
Pokeweed
Thistles
Wild grapes
Sour grass/wood sorrel
Rock tripe
Milkweed
Lamb's quarters
Arrow leaf
Arrow leaf roots
Water lily
Water lily root
Daylily
Ginseng

NUTS

Hickory nut
Acorn
Beach nut
Black walnut
White walnut
Chestnut
Hazel nuts

Fruits

Pawpaw
Persimmon
Apple
Berries
Wine berries

DR. RUSSELL JONES

Blackberry
Raspberry
Serviceberry
Huckleberry
Wild blueberry
Elderberry

19

WHAT IS WOO?

Woo is the paranormal aspect of Bigfoot research. Think cloaking, portals, aliens, UFOs, mind speak, zapping, etc. I bet for a lot of people reading this book, it's shocking that some people believe there could be any of those things related to Bigfoot. The vast majority of Bigfoot researchers believe that Bigfoot is some type of undiscovered hominid species. A primate.

Say ten to fifteen years ago, we never really heard of much of this aspect of Bigfoot. There might have been a few people around, like noted Bigfoot researcher Thom Powell, looking at odd cases, but it really wasn't even really talked about. Now, visit social media or the internet, and it's full of discussion of these topics.

From a personal perspective, the part of woo that I have experienced is the belief that Bigfoot could somehow affect electronics. There's part of me that knows some people can't wear watches and other similar things like that because of their personal chemistry, but it's clearly rare. Bigfoot researcher Darren Pevarnik and I were the only humans for miles in a remote location. He had set up his thermal to watch our campsite while we slept. I could hear things moving around all night, and audio confirmed something was there.

In fact, audio heard something pick up an OFF! Can (bug spray) and literally grunt. In the morning when Darren went to check the footage of the thermal, it said it "couldn't format". That was the first and last time that ever happened.

The author has found many unusual things in his treks throughout Appalachia.

The other instance is when I was using game cameras in a great spot. A very deep creek that must be swum to cross and cliffs at the top of the hill. I used two cameras to block the hillside. Nothing could get past without being on film. Well, both cameras functioned normally till the second week of December, then shut off till the second week of April when they turned on at the same time. I sent both cameras to Reconyx, who said they were functioning normally. I have had other cameras over the years that haven't taken as many pictures as they should have.

The reality is it's hard to implement technology in the field with wide varied weather conditions most likely affecting sensitive electronics. I have yet in my lifelong time in the woods have anything happen to me that I couldn't explain by natural means.

This 24x32 picture was propped up against a tree and found in a remote location off trail.

I've said this many times and in many places: woo is lazy. It's attaching the paranormal to something that isn't probable in the minds of many. I believe that there are scientists interested in the

Bigfoot phenomena but are scared of how some of the citizen science is being conducted and the paranormal aspect of Bigfoot. Most of our citizen researchers are spending very little time in the woods and are not woodsmen. They don't understand the animals and their habits, don't know the trees, plants, or ecology. They don't know how to track. They are most often found on trails. That is why Bigfoot seems paranormal to them. If they feel funny in the woods at night, in a place they seldom go, with only a red light, they have been "zapped". Zapped being Bigfoot sending ultra or subsonic waves at them to disorient them.

Infrasound is a real thing that elephants, tigers, lions, and some other things we don't know about use. For predators the belief is that it stuns the prey for an instant so they can be caught. For non-prey animals? Who knows, probably some form of communication.

The point here being that the answer is usually the easiest and clearest, the most likely if you will. In these cases, it's most likely stress and anxiety. You're in a place that has a history of Bigfoot activity, it's dark, isolated, and you're on edge, maybe tired. The point is to follow science. Is it possible that Bigfoot uses infrasound? Sure, and we may find that out later. It's best to follow what is most likely even if you don't like how it makes you sound.

In the last thirty years of seeing patients, over two hundred thousand visits, I've taken great joy in asking old-timers and hunters, "What is the weirdest thing you have seen in the woods?" or "Have you ever been afraid in the woods?" Most people who are woodsmen are candid, have had weird experiences, and have been uneasy or even afraid. So if these people who are in the woods over a lifetime have had it happen, why wouldn't you?

*Right of ways can serve as passageways for game and provide
edge to attract game.*

I believe that woo is going to expand and sadly become more prevalent. People aren't becoming more woods savvy. Some of the woo believers are compelling, and who doesn't like a good mystery? I'm not saying don't listen and document their story; you should, that's part of science. I'm saying that in many cases there is most likely a natural explanation.

20

MY MUSINGS

Everyone who is interested in Bigfoot, whether an author, researcher, or an enthusiast, has thoughts in general about groupings or smaller topics that many times have no sure answer but are interesting nonetheless, such as the difference between the east coast and west coast bigfooting.

In terms of Bigfoot, the east coast is the stepchild. The subject was taken much more seriously earlier and was more accepting by the residents on the west coast. For many decades the researchers on the west coast found the claims of Bigfoot sightings on the east coast dubious. As recently as ten years ago, I can still remember researchers finding the east coast claims suspect. If you think about how Bigfoot got here, it makes sense. Whatever Bigfoot is, it came across the Bering Strait ten thousand to twenty thousand years ago. It spread out across North America, following game and in search of territory. It makes sense that the top three states in the US for sightings are in the Pacific Northwest. Number four, though, is Ohio, and that really threw a monkey wrench in things early on. Some famous Bigfooters, such as Matt Moneymaker, founder of the BFRO and its important database that all researchers at, first investigated in Ohio and had a sighting there.

It's rare to see a Bigfoot on open ground in Appalachia. Much of the leaf duff makes finding them a challenge.

Our west coast brethren tend to be more secretive and don't share information as much as is done on the east coast. I suspect that it's so competitive out there. Personally, I can tell you that when I call or message out west, help can be tentative, whereas on the east coast, the great majority of researchers will help in any way.

When leading expeditions on the east coast, we schedule around a full moon, believing it affects Bigfoot movement; the west coast schedules the opposite.

All of the Bigfoot legend stories, such as the Patterson-Gimlin film, Ruby Creek, etc., come from out west. About a third of the Bigfoot reports come from out west. About a third of the people in the United States believe in Bigfoot, but it's much higher in the Pacific Northwest.

Another quandary is why do some states that you wouldn't suspect have such high Bigfoot sightings? Of course, when considering sighting numbers, most people will look at the BFRO database. The BFRO has trained investigators in each state who vet the reports that come in. Some states have few or no investigators, think Idaho, Maine, and Montana. I remember many times members of the BFRO from other states would help out in states like that. As another example, I'm sure that Bigfoot may be in Utah, there may be some reports, but there are few researchers there compared to other states. In other places like Illinois or Kentucky, most would find it shocking that they would be in the top ten in sightings. The reality is both of those states have one really active researcher. They do a great job and follow up on almost every report, driving these states higher on the list. West Virginia, which is seventeenth, has a small resident population and some of the harshest terrain in the United States. It has few researchers; I suspect the actual Bigfoot numbers may be much higher than represented. Ohio has a Bigfoot culture similar to the Pacific Northwest. It hosts the largest Bigfoot conference and has many similar events. It has many Bigfoot researchers. I suggest that a higher percentage of Bigfoot encounters get documented than in other states. So many of the numbers that suggest actual likelihood of Bigfoot or encountering them are driven by factors other than reality.

Rocky overhangs are many times old mines throughout Appalachia.

What time of the year has the most sightings? Well, of course you must have a Bigfoot and a witness to have a sighting. More people are out in the summer, and thus so are the majority of the sightings. Fall is not far behind, and I suspect the leaves being off of the trees allows a prospective witness a greater field and space of vision. While hunters are out in greater numbers in the field, by sheer volume of people, summer wins. This tells me that being in the woods and actually being a hunter or acting like one may lead to the greatest opportunity for a sighting. That means slowly walking through the woods or sitting quietly and not moving. Of course, this assumes we are in a place with a history of Bigfoot sightings. In all likelihood choosing a state like Ohio in Appalachia, which hold some large areas but not in the amounts found in places like West Virginia, Kentucky, or Tennessee, may lead to an advantage. Think fishing in a pond versus the ocean. Sadly, you're not trying to just catch just a fish in the pond but the rarest one!

21

WHAT I THINK I KNOW

I think there are a lot of people out there with pictures, videos, maybe even bones right now. When a body is collected or Bigfoot is verified, a lot of people will come forward with evidence. I believe that some people worry about being laughed at, and others don't want the Bigfoot they see around their property bothered.

I remember getting an excited phone call from Caroline, the secretary of the BFRO; she had a witness that was close to me. The witness was a veterinarian and had a farm. Part of the year she was getting glimpses of a family of Bigfoot (she assumed). She had been collecting some evidence. Before I could even call her, she had called back and said she had decided that she didn't want people on her land or people bothering the animals. That was years ago, and I still think about it. She was only a few miles from my house. If you're reading this, let's please talk.

I think that the Bigfoot enigma may be solved at literally any time. I expect it to be sooner than later. That being said, several years ago I was talking to Monongahela, the sound recording expert that many researchers across the country use, and I predicted the same.

A 6' by 6' possible Bigfoot bed, padded by leaves, high on a hillside overlooking the only entrance to a remote valley and creek.

I think that woo is going to be less involved in the Bigfoot mystery when it's all said and done. I've written at length about woo in another chapter. I believe that people use it as a way of explaining the things they can't explain or that their skill set doesn't explain. I'm not saying don't investigate the reports that may sound "wooish"; we should document everything.

I think the high-tech toys we are employing and developing will lead to more anecdotal evidence. It will be compelling but still not largely accepted by mainstream science. It's a body, or a piece of one, that's needed, period. It reminds me of politics, everyone saying on both sides, "It's the economy, stupid!" In this case, "It's the Bigfoot, stupid!"

I think that the federal government knows more about Bigfoot than what they let on in public. I'm a moderate conspiracy theorist, I mean I believe Bigfoot exists. The government may not believe the public is capable of handling this truth, and after Covid, I suspect they may be correct.

I think that most sightings and interactions may be adolescents, MOST.

Walking remote waterways in times of droughts may produce track finds.

I think that Bigfoot may live closer to us than many of us would believe. After all, humans, while dangerous, are associated with food.

I think that while humans look similar, we look different. I think Bigfoot is the same. Maybe it's a regional difference or some subspecies or intermingling. If you look through the reports, it seems clear that their body types, including the head shape, vary.

I think that more weight should be given to eyewitness testimony. Historically humans have been considered poor eyewitnesses, especially when it comes to height and weight. Humans have not been a bad witness when considering if something is human. That's a pretty low bar for witnesses. Additionally, the sheer volume of reports add up. Throw away all the bad and/or sketchy witnesses, keep only the most awesome ones, and the public would be shocked to know how many exceptional reports there are by professionals and trained observers.

22

WHAT I KNOW

I know that the rarity of the creature is the central part of the challenge of documenting. Humans are in the woods less now than ever, and with fewer outdoor skills. People who have ever tried to find a lost rabbit or coon hound might grasp the dilemma. Dogs have less intelligence than a primate, and dogs being attracted to houses are still hard to find. Humans also largely stay on trails and follow the easiest paths. I remember one time I was bow hunting and was one hundred yards from a right-of-way. I could hear a four-wheeler coming when I saw four deer. They ran about fifty feet into woods from the right-of-way and held still. The four-wheeler passed, having no idea the deer were in the area. I know animals do this.

I know that Bigfoot isn't making as many tree structures as many would have you believe. Our forefathers were skilled woodsmen and would have hunted these animals down if they were leaving them commonly. We've talked about how many of the supposed structures are pines. Pines have a weak root structure and fly all around during storms. There is evidence of higher primates manipulating trees, shrubs, and bushes, so it seems reasonable that Bigfoot would as well. Bigfoot, having remained so elusive and hidden for all these years, makes it also seem reasonable that I have said many times, "Bigfoot is rare and so is evidence of their passing."

The author believes that Bigfoot are opportunistic, omnivore, ambush predators with a high intelligence. They are not a dumb ape.

I know that there is enough food to provide enough sustenance for a creature the size of Bigfoot. Many naturalists like myself have visited this question over the years, and it's been decided scientifically. Occasionally on TV or a podcast I may hear an individual postulate that it's not true, but at this point I suspect they are just trying to click-bait to drive interest and numbers.

I know there are more encounters taking place than people realize. I have said before that you must be able to recognize the sounds and behaviors to realize an encounter. I know that before I knew anything about Bigfoot, I had several encounters, as did family members, and didn't recognize it. On hearing wood knocks deep in the wilderness of Southeastern Ohio, my grandfather, who was the most knowledgeable woodsman I knew, believed the sounds to be a car door slamming way down the "holler", and the sound carries funny. He just didn't know that there was such a thing in the woods. Just last year I was in the woods with my uncle, and we were walking up a horribly thick drain when I noticed a nest of sorts that had quite a few branches about wrist thick twisted off lying on it. I said, "Look at this," and he just kind of shrugged. It wasn't related to anything that we were after, so it wasn't given much pause. I know that if you gave our older woodsmen the knowledge of Bigfoot, many of them have had experiences.

I know that not everything in the woods is Bigfoot behavior. Too many of our researchers and habituators begin to make every noise or "thing" that happens in the woods Bigfoot. Bigfoot is rare, not everywhere; if it weren't so, it wouldn't be a mystery or controversy at this point.

I know Bigfoot is curious and cautious. They don't feel the need to have to come in because we are frying bacon. Many times, in very rural places in Appalachia, they would just as soon move back as interact. We are best served to be in a place or doing something they are not used to seeing or experiencing.

23

BEST OF APPALACHIA BIGFOOT
REPORTS

There are literally thousands of Bigfoot reports around. I have chosen these, as they show something different in Bigfoot behavior or sometimes commonalities in behavior. Most of the reports have come from the BFRO database, some published and some that have never been seen. I appreciate my friend and director of the BFRO, Matt Moneymaker, always helping me with access and thoughts on different cases. In most cases I have retroactively reached out to the witness and/or researcher for thoughts not originally included. I believe all of these cases to be true. I have in cases slightly altered a location or name in order to protect the public.

∽

Year: 2010
Season: Fall
Month: October
State: Ohio
County: Fairfield
Location: Clear Creek Park

Observed: On Saturday, October 9th, 2010, I was finishing up a senior photo shoot at Lake Ramona on Clear Creek Road in Fairfield County. Upon arrival at the lake, immediately we observed rocks being thrown into the lake. There were three of us who witnessed it, my wife and young son had gone up another trail and were no longer present with us. My photo subject and I had gone to the lower area to try to get a few shots, but the rock throwing continued. Also observed was tree knocking and limb breaking by the creature at this time and when we moved back to where we originally heard it. We were across the lake from it, and that time I decided to take a succession of pictures to try and find what was throwing rocks at us. At this point in time, all of us decided to leave the area, since I had my wife and young son with me. I didn't want to run a risk of them getting hurt. It was when I got home that I realized I had actually gotten two images of the creature. I also believe that I have another of it observing me when I was taking a picture of the boy in front of the lake, but it's not as clear as the other two. To me in the photos its face resembled an orangutan, only it was completely Black. Also of interest is that the creature appears to have something white in its hand.

Also Noticed: There was a smaller black shape in a tree, but I was unable to determine whether it was a young creature. It was impossible to determine the sex of the creature so there was no way of tell if it was a mother protecting its offspring.

Other Witnesses: Myself, the young man I was photographing, and his father.

Other Stories: According to a friend of mine living in the area, they have heard unusual screams.

Time and Condition: This happened around noon, the day was sunny, and it was unseasonably warm.

Landscape: Sighting occurred directly across the lake. There was a small footbridge that we had to cross and a small hill we had to climb in order to get to the lake.

Follow-up Investigation Report by BFRO Investigator Dr. Russ Jones: I met with the witness and investigator Brad Kennan at the location on November 28. I had already talked to the witness by phone shortly after he had filed the report. We had, prior to going to the sighting location, had the photographs analyzed by members of the BFRO to make sure there had been no tampering and to try to get a better look at the images.

This incident took place at Clear Creek Park, which is a five-thousand-acre portion of the Columbus Metro Park System. This portion is just south of Lancaster, Ohio. While the park itself is not large, it is located in the Hocking Hills region of Southeastern Ohio. It is very close to Wahkeena Nature Preserve, Old Man's Cave State Park, and is just a couple of miles from Wayne National Forest. The park itself is the farthest southern reaches of the glaciers, providing rich flat bottoms surrounded by hardwood forests. There is one main road that runs through the park. The sighting took place at Lake Ramona, which is a five-acre lake. In order to access the lake, you must first park and then walk in. If anyone else is in the area, it would be readily apparent.

After viewing the pictures, talking to this witness, and realizing there had been several other reports within two miles of this location, we went to go and take measurements and get a better idea of the terrain. After reviewing the pictures and being at the location, investigator Brad Kennan and I can agree on the following: The location has a history of Bigfoot sightings; this area is a prime territory for these creatures to exist; the witness was sincere and believable; stick breaking and rock throwing is behavior often reported during Sasquatch encounters. We find the pictures inconclusive. They do resemble a lot of the pictures around the country and may very well show a Bigfoot; it's just impossible for us to say with any certainty. Nonetheless, the pictures are included for the public's own evaluations and opinions. It should be noted that his three photos were taken as he held his camera up with his arm extended, one picture right after another, at the directions the noises were coming from. We have not included the picture of the boy having his senior pictures taken. The background in the picture is not very clear and not worth the boy's privacy.

Afterthoughts: Like so many witnesses, a person who is living their normal busy life with no thoughts of Bigfoot becomes consumed with it afterwards. I often see this witness at Bigfoot conferences now. Having a Bigfoot encounter is life changing on many fronts.

On another note, Matt Moneymaker sent me a well-known wildlife scent maker who had an interest in Bigfoot. He had developed a sexual primate scent/pheromone mixture and a curiosity scent aimed at Bigfoot. I chose this general area for the experiment. We put two game cameras one hundred yards apart with cleared spots in front of each. The scent maker stayed three days doctoring the spots and then left a long-term dripper over each. I left cameras in place for over a year and didn't get a shot. Was it in the wrong place? Was the camera heard? Did the scent not last long enough to be present when and/or if a Bigfoot was around? At present we are working on a different delivery system. Once again, improvise and come up with new ideas.

One other interesting note is that this area is a sanctuary, meaning that there are few trails and use is restricted to them. It gives an animal such as Bigfoot a lot more room for safety and privacy. Just like a big buck moving to an area that doesn't allow hunting during hunting season. I believe Bigfoot uses posted land, sanctuaries, and no-hunting land inside state parks as well as remote land that no one goes on.

~

Year: 2006/2007
Season: Fall

Month: November
Date: Tuesday before Thanksgiving
State: West Virginia
County: Roane
Nearest Town: Walton

Observed: It was on a Tuesday before Thanksgiving back in 2006. My son was playing just over the ridge with his dog. The ridge was only about 20-30 yards from our cabin. It was clear and sunny and around noon. I was making lunch for him and me so we could get back in the woods deer hunting. He came running and screaming there was a big black hairy man walking around down by the oil wells. I just said yeah ok, come eat lunch. My dad was with us, and he and my son stayed at the cabin while I went back out deer hunting. When I got back to the cabin, I asked my dad "how did you like your walk back up the creek?" He told me that he and my son had laid down for a nap and that my son was still sleeping. A year later I found a hidden cave entrance in the side of one of the ridges on the property. About 10-15 feet from that entrance, I found three nearly identical piles of scat. One pile very fresh, on pile partly dry, and the third crusty dry. The size of the turds are what scared the hell out of me. They were about as big around as a tennis ball and 9-12 inches long. Not bear scat and the piles were in a line like the same animal went to poop there three different times. I'm a country boy. Raised hunting, fishing, and trapping. I know most all the animals in the woods, and none have piles of scat this big. I saw something walk up the ridge towards the cemetery and it wasn't my dad or son.

Also Noticed: My son saw it first. I saw it later that afternoon around sunset. Later there were stones thrown at us around a campfire. We found the scat piles later. Then the following spring is when I found the stripped deer carcass.

Other Stories: The following spring I went up the cabin to meet with a timber man about thinning our trees. While down by the oil wells we found a stripped deer carcass. The weird thing was that both front hooves had been broken off and missing. That's when the hair on the back of my neck stood up so hard that it hurt.

Landscape: rolling hills, bluffs, and creek bottom. Very rural! Mixed hardwood into pine depending upon whether you are going uphill or downhill toward the creek bottom.

Afterthoughts: One of many reports that I never got to meet the gentleman. In my notes it said I couldn't reach him. Looking back now, I suspect there may be a reason that I didn't just drive up there hoping to find the place. The gentleman was meeting with timber people in 2007, and I suppose that like so many times, the environment changed. He filed a report thirteen years after the incident, and clearly not much else had happened, or it would have been mentioned.

This may be a prime example of the "halibut effect". Those fish can be found repeatedly over the years if the conditions are largely the same. It appears the same with Bigfoot. One of the areas I've just now begun working is because of this. In the 1970s there were a lot of reports, and the area is probably better now than it was back then, so there's a good chance that something could be around. Another consideration is the move away from "ambulance chasing". That, of course, is running around after each report that comes in, especially when it's been years since the incident. Many, many Bigfoot researchers, including myself, have done this, and it's a waste of time.

∾

Year: 2009
Season: Fall
Month: October
State: West Virginia
County: McDowell

Nearest Town: Bradshaw

Observed: My friend Corey and I decided to go bow hunting one day in the fall of October 2009 in the mountains behind our houses. We came to a big brush pile which we couldn't be seen from the direction we were headed. We had thought we saw someone else that was hunting coming our way from the direction we couldn't be seen but the closer it got the more unusual it got. It was walking about 50 yards below us and when we finally got a good look at if we could see it was a Bigfoot. It was about 8-10 feet tall, fur from head to toe, and was extremely thick and muscular. We watched in amazement as it walked for about 100 yards and then was out of sight. We told all of our friends about it and got interest from them as well. We went back the next weekend with 6 of us in total at about the same time that we had seen it. We went to the same path it was traveling and kept hearing something in the distance on the same path ahead of us, so we decided to try and track it in two separate groups. On the path we found two separate footprints that were human like but huge. We also kept hearing something ahead of us the entire time. We got to the top of the mountain ridge when the sun was starting to set and while we were talking all 6 of us saw the Bigfoot heading down the other side of the ridge.

Other Stories: Yes, my football coach had told me after I spoke of my incident that he had heard one yelling right next to his property years before which had extremely frightened him. Apparently, there have been sightings in Panther State Forest which is close to him and 2 ridges over from where I had seen mine.

Landscape: mountains

Investigator Commentary by Matt Moneymaker: I spoke with the primary witness by phone. He is now 28 years old and lives in North Carolina. He grew up in the area where the incidents occurred. At the time he was a teenager and so were the other witnesses. Note:

Most rural teenagers did not have smartphones in 2009. They didn't carry cameras like they all do today. His grandfather still lives at the West Virginia property. Also noted: When the six of them saw the Bigfoot walking away from them over the ridge it was approximately 40 yards away and was fleeing them. That visual incident didn't last nearly as long as the visual incident the prior weekend where they were looking over the hill at the Bigfoot. At the closest point it was 50 yards away. They watched it walk for about 100 yards until it was out of their view. When they returned the following weekend, the purpose was to show their friends. Taking photos wasn't as important as simply showing their friends. Today it would be different. Don't make assumptions about what should have occurred with some rural teens in 2009, and what they should have been carrying with them.

Afterthoughts: It's hard to imagine how steep the mountains are in some places in southern West Virginia. I remember when first viewing the steepness thinking I didn't know how the trees were able to grow. I remember hearing a story about Panther Creek State Park relayed by a state policeman that there was a family reunion of about thirty people who saw a Bigfoot walk close to where they were all at. The relatives from Ohio thought it was a prank! The park being just two ridges over from the sighting above. Some of these locations in West Virginia prove very hard to even get to, and the locals can be suspicious of outsiders. I hate to feed the stereotype by saying that, but as a resident, I guess I'm entitled to.

～

Year: 1987
Season: Summer
Month: July
State: West Virginia
County: Tucker
Nearest town: Davis

Observed: Dear Sirs, On July 4, 1987, Saturday evening about 11:30 pm, myself and two others had a close-up visual sighting of 2 Bigfoot. I was standing inches away from my friend when we both encountered this. I grew up spending a lot more time in the woods than most of my associates and have seen countless bear and cats in the wild. I was never so scared of anything in my life as I was that night. The thing that over-whelmed me was when I shined the flashlight in its face, the eyes were yellow, the exact same color as deer's eyes at night. That told me this thing was nocturnal. I would be forever trying to write everything down that happened that night, so I would like to speak to someone that is highly experienced in this field.

Also Noticed: The one myself and my friend witnessed walked with a limp. It looked like it was dragging its right leg as it walked.

Conditions: three-quarter moon. Perfectly clear. 67 degrees.

Other Witnesses: Three of us witnessed 2 different Bigfoot at the same time walking in opposite directions.

Landscape: This area is about 40 some years old. There was a large fire here in the 1940's or so. The new growth consists mainly of pine trees. There is a stream at the sighting. This was on top of a mountain.

Investigator Commentary by Dan Nedrelo: The three men have told very few people. Whatever it was looked like a human being in the distance. Close-up, the hair made details of its face hard to observe. It was heavy, wide, and the specimen observed by the two men appeared to have one leg dragging. Upon approaching very close, perhaps nine feet away, it turned off the trail, crossed a meadow, and went into heavy brush. They did not follow. On the phone the brother who submitted the report said to me, "This was the most incredible thing I have seen in my life." One of the unwritten laws in this area is you don't mess with people who are armed. Glimpses of whatever was in camp with them from time to time were made by the father. He spent one night in his truck because of what were described as violent screams. He had active duty in Vietnam and was thoroughly comfortable in the woods.

Afterthoughts: I can also add that the witness was a successful businessman. He observed the animal with a "Neanderthal type body for about twenty seconds". Bigfoot sightings can happen most anywhere, but some locations make it much more likely. This location has almost the most Bigfoot sightings though it is one of the least populated areas in the east coast. I took the *Finding Bigfoot* television show here, and they had a lot of action in the area.

Year: 1969
Season: Fall
Month: August
State: West Virginia
County: McDowell
Nearest town: War

Observed: The year was 1969. It was a very dry August. My sister and I were going to the store. She chose to walk the way of the dirt road and I chose to walk down the path from my grandparents' home up on the side of a hill. I was watching my sister from up on the path as she walked the road, approximately 200 yards above her. When she passed the well, a natural spring, this creature stood up. It was tall, broad shouldered, with arms hanging below its knees. It was hairy but not thick hair; I could see the skin on its back. I screamed for my sister to run, she turned toward me, saw the creature, and ran. I can still see the dust rise from her feet as she ran. This creature immediately stooped back down and entered the brush alongside the creek below me. It moved faster than anything that large should be able to move. We told our grandmother, she said it had always been there and was just getting water. She also said that her mean old bear dogs were scared to come out from under the house whenever it was around. She said it like to wander around on damp rainy nights. This is no hoax. I am a science major, a registered nurse, who remembers the incident that cannot be explained unless Bigfoot is real. I believe that we saw Bigfoot and I believes he still lives up Shop Hollow, Slate Creek Area in Mcdowell County.

Also Noticed: told stories from other mountain people. I was told it was unusual that this creature was out in broad daylight.

Conditions: About Noon or 1300, hot and unusually dry with no rain. The creek had dried up, that I remember.

Landscape: Mountain area, sparsely populated.

Investigator Commentary by Dr. Russ Jones: I talked with the witness, a fifty-year-old ER nurse, about her experience that happened when she was nine years old. She described the creature as "gangly". It was at least seven feet tall with reddish brown hair. The hair was longer on the shoulders and back and thin enough in some spots to see through. Compared to a human, the arms were longer in proportion. This is a very rural area in the southernmost portion of West Virginia, with steep, rugged, rocky, and inhospitable terrain. She mentioned many old mine openings in addition to caves.

Afterthoughts: I remember even though it was years ago how adamant this witness was. She remembers her and her sister both crying. She saw the creature from the side and could see ears. Her father had claimed to see a smaller, darker Bigfoot run up a hill in front of him on all fours ten years prior. I've always loved doing these old reports. Not only do they establish a history of Bigfoot sightings, the witnesses seem to be more sincere. It's always important to consider extremes in the weather like cold, wet, dry, etc. I know the driest month in West Virginia is September, and when it's dry, I always try to hike near water.

∽

Year: 1979
Season: Spring
Month: May
State: Ohio
County: Hocking
Nearest Town: Haydenville

Observed: In 1979, my family and I lived on a farm in Haydenville, Ohio, just outside of Logan, Ohio. My dad had just painted our front porch, so we had to go out the back door to feed our dog named Wolf (he was tied up in the front yard). One particular night, my dad sent my brother Jim out the back door to go feed Wolf. Jim was 10 years old at the time and not afraid of anything. So, he got some water and headed out back to feed the dog (now first of all, I need to explain if you stood at the back door in the kitchen you could walk straight through to our living room where my mom was sitting on the couch). Just as soon as Jim opened the back door, he dropped the water and slammed the door and ran straight to our mom on the couch and jumped on her lap. He acted like he couldn't talk. My dad came running in the room and started patting him on the face to get him to talk. Finally, all my brother could say was big, hairy, and building. He was too shocked to say anymore. After a few moments he finally told my dad that there was a big hairy man leaning against the building out back. The building was at least six feet tall, and Jim said it was leaning on it with its elbow! After hearing this, my dad opened the front door and jumped over the porch, and ran to our dog, untied him, and the ran out back. Wolf ran ahead but dad didn't get far. He was halfway there and heard Wolf cry then flew past dad! Whatever it was, it slapped our dog making him fly past my dad! So, dad ran down to the garage to get some neighbor boys and their guns and they chased it back into the woods. We thought that was the end of it, but it wasn't. The very next night dad was in the garage fixing a car. Mom was putting my younger brothers and sisters to bed upstairs. Me and my other sister Donna were downstairs in our bedroom (which was right by the back door). We had just gone into bed when I looked over and it was looking in our bedroom window!! I was stunned. I told my sister and we had to get upstairs to mom and be very quiet. When he left our window, we got up and started out the door where we could see it at the back door trying to get in. We ran upstairs and told our mom. She says we were nuts since they chased it away last night. She started downstairs but only got so far down before she ran back up knocking me and my sister over. Mom ran to the window and started screaming for dad yelling it's at the back door!!! This time my mom called the sheriff. When they arrived, they went through the woods looking for it. All they found was where it had apparently thrown up and the acid burned the ground. Heck the sheriffs wouldn't even go further than the light of the farmhouse! After that, we never seen it again. I never told this story to anyone but friends and family because quite frankly, I really don't think anyone would believe me. By the way the creature was probably seven feet tall or better. You could tell it had black hair, but it had lots of gray hair too. It looked very old. He looked like a man in the face but much bigger. It was very scary looking.

Conditions: Around 9pm. Nice spring night.

Landscape: Wayne National Forest was our backyard.

Investigator Commentary by Marc DeWerth: The witness described the face as very manlike except for the hair, which did not cover the cheeks, eyes, and nose. The eyes gleamed a reddish color. The hair was dark in color and appeared to be gray or silver tipped on the head and chest area. Looking at it made the witness feel that this particular creature was very old. It had a really rugged look about it with lots of wrinkles. The door handle did jiggle like the creature was trying to open the door, which made the family think it was trying to get in the back door to look for food. The sheriff's department acted scared to death and wouldn't go into the woods even though they were armed. It was never seen again after the second instance. It could have been sick. They think the acid on the ground was from the creature vomiting.

Afterthoughts: There are still reports in the area today. What a scary sighting. There are many reports where witnesses had the impression that the animal was old and as a result displayed behavior not consistent with what was considered typical, such as eating corn at a deer feeder with a camera aimed at it, as was seen in another case where the witness believed the Bigfoot to be older.

Year: 2013
Season: Summer
Month: July
State: Ohio
County: Athens
Nearest town: Nelsonville

Observed: I decided to go primitive camping by myself at Wayne National Forest which is a place that I've never been. My plan was to camp from July 22-24. Unfortunately, the time off work I scheduled ended up being preceded by many days of heavy rain, and the first day I went to Wayne was no different. I picked up a topo map from the local ranger's office, and with the help of a person at the office I picked a location to camp. The location was about a mile and a half down a trail near a pond. By the time I hiked to the location I picked on the map (1pm), I was thoroughly soaked. Wading through wet foliage and the constant rain soaked me pretty good. I set up a camp on a flat spot along a hill with a pond downhill, a ridge uphill, and a gully a little further ahead. During the rain, I basically heard nothing and saw no animals. I just hung out under my cover which was a large poncho I used as a tarp. Finally, the rain stopped at about 5:30 pm. I went down the hill to see if I could catch any fish. I caught a few small fish. I fished for a while, and then went back to my camp to try to make a fire around 630 pm. I brought tinder (cotton balls), but because of the ground, the air, and everything was so wet, I could not get a fire started. I continuously tried to get a fire started from 630 pm to 715 pm. From about 6:45 to 7:45 is when my experience occurred. I first heard knocking coming from somewhere past the gully. It was several knocks, but I wasn't concerned because it could have been many things causing a knocking sound—a woodpecker, etc. Next, about ten minutes later, I heard something large slowly moving in the undergrowth which was on the opposite side of me from the gully and downhill from the ridge. I was a little concerned because I had no doubt it was an animal of some kind. Just a few minutes later, I heard what I can best describe as a "slide whistle" sound coming from near where I heard the movement in the undergrowth. I was a little concerned at that point. I've never heard an animal make that kind of sound. Several minutes later, something "fell" from atop the ridge above me. I didn't see it, but it was large enough to make a substantial noise as it came down the hill. I say, "fell" because it did not seem to come straight down as in a tree branch falling straight down from a tree. It seemed to have a trajectory that followed along the hill. Keep in mind that during this whole time is when I was attempting to make a fire. The next thing that occurred, along with not being able to make a fire, made me think I should give up the idea of camping and leave. I heard loud leaf rustling on top of the ridge. It was so loud, I thought for sure something was going to come running down the hill, so I looked up toward the ridge. What I saw took me a moment to understand. I saw the top portion of a tree, the canopy, shaking back and forth violently. Only the one tree was shaking. It was shaking, not swaying. The weather was fine at the moment. There was no apparent wind or rain. No other tree was moving. This tree was likely the thickness of a utility pole at its base. It was not a small tree. It shook for about 20 second's total. I had experienced enough at that point, so I quickly as I could packed up my poncho, etc. and headed back out of the woods. I've seen enough Bigfoot shows and have read enough to know that people believe much of what I experienced up to this point is characteristic of Bigfoot encounters. I quickly made my way back to the trail which ended about 50 yards from my campsite. The foliage is thick on both sides for most of the trail, so I couldn't see very far off of the trail. That unnerved me a bit, so despite being concerned that something was in the woods, I stopped several times on the way out of the woods to make sure that nothing was following me. Three times, on the way out, I smelled something rotten, which I've heard is characteristic of Bigfoot encounters. So, each time I stopped, listened, and looked around. The smell could have been simply rotten vegetation. I don't know. I periodically scanned the top of the ridge, when I could see it, because I assumed that if something was following me, it might be following me along the ridge. This would likely be true of a predator type animal. The ridge is a good vantage point. The third time that I smelled something there was a small break along my right side and up a small gulley. I had a clear view to the top of the ridge, so I stood still for a moment and looked at the top of the ridge which was easily two hundred feet away at that point. My eye quickly caught movement just down from the ridge. At first, I thought it was a person. It was moving in the same direction I had been going. When I first caught a glimpse of it out of the corner of my eye (so to speak), I saw what I thought was arm swing. That's why I first thought it was a person. But once I fixed my eyes on it, all that I saw was a vertical figure moving straight across the hill with no arm swing. I only saw the top portion of the figure for a second or so because the foliage along the trail in this area was too dense and too high other than the small break. The figure stood vertically, not horizontally like an animal. It moved linearly which seemed very odd. The brief second I saw it clearly, it moved straight across, not up and down as a person running would. I did not see any arm swing again. I still can't explain how it moved in such a straight line along a hill. I did not see any features. I believe I was looking at it from the side, so it looked narrow just as a person would if you looked at a person from the side. The figure was light gray, but even from a distance I could see that the gray was more of a "salt and pepper" gray. I could see that the hair ran down the length of the figure vertically. I saw that it was not a uniform gray, much like a rabbit is not uniform in color. It had strands of darker hair running vertically. The darker areas could have been wet areas. I don't know. I took off as quick as I could. I can't say if it was a Bigfoot because I don't know if they really exist. Whatever it was, it was as least as big as a person, and not like any animal I had ever seen.

Investigator Commentary by Dr. Russ Jones: This witness is a bright well-spoken lawyer who is an experienced outdoorsman. I spoke to him several times about the incident and find his experience compelling. I went to the location and spent several hours hiking around and looking at the areas he mentioned. I also put a game camera out. The witness in the end believes he had a Bigfoot encounter.

Afterthoughts: I left the camera out over a year and didn't have anything Bigfoot related on the pictures, sadly. In the more recent past the area had received four-wheeler traffic, so it may not be as good as what it once was in terms of Bigfoot activity. I have taken several reports within a few miles of this encounter.

Concerning the smell often associated with Bigfoot sightings. About 15% of Bigfoot sightings are associated with a smell. Higher apes have a gland called the apocrine gland, which is mostly in the armpit or groin area and often gives off a scent if the animal is frightened or excited.

~

Year: 2004
Season: Summer
Month: June
State: Ohio
County: Vinton
Nearest Town: McArthur

Observed: On June 20, 2004, at 2 AM, I was lounging in my recliner watching TV. I noticed something like a large dark shadow looking in my window. We have four full length windows with no curtains because our windows face the woods. I had no lights on other than the TV and my fish aquarium. The moon was slightly giving some light but not enough to make out any features. At first, I thought I was just imagining this. Slowly, I turned off the TV. When I did, the shadow moved over. I thought it was my imagination, so I covered my head and went to sleep in my recliner. The next morning at 6 AM, I was still unnerved. When I looked toward the window, there was two large handprints on the glass about 12 inches long. My brother wears a size 14 ring, and these fingers were about four inches longer than his hand. It looked like a very large man's hand with fingers spread apart. I am retired from a police department and worked in fingerprinting and latent examination. I called my two brothers t come to my house and went into the bedroom to wake up my husband. I trembled in fear for about an hour afterwards. This thing had to be at least eight to nine feet tall to be standing where it was. I showed the handprints to my entire family. I did not want to report this because I am a foster parent, and I was afraid of people thinking I was crazy. On July 20, 2004, my dogs were screaming wildly. That night, my brother had stayed over since he was sick and was sleeping in the spare bedroom. At 4 AM, something was beating on the walls so hard that it knocked items off of a shelf over the bed and dislodged my vinyl siding. This was new siding just installed in the spring! Needless to say, we were up all night. I was talking to my brother a few nights later at around 1 AM when I noticed another set of handprints on the window. Being a trained fingerprint technician, they appeared to not be human and showed very little detail at all. The next day, we decided to clean these prints off of our windows. We figured whatever had left them would be back and leave some more. We used pure vinegar to clean the prints. Whatever was on its hands did not want to come off! It took some serous scrubbing to finally remove them. Other than the handprints, my windows were actually very clean. I have lived here for four years. My foster daughters told us that twice that they were seeing a big man around our 1.5-acre pond. I didn't believe it was anything like this! We live in the country. Ever since we bought a large dog kennel to keep the dogs from running around, this thing is brave enough to look in the windows and hit the house. I am convinced that something is outside my house. We live very close to Zaleski State Forest. We will be setting up brother in laws wildlife camera hoping to catch this thing on film. I will let you know if and when we get a picture.

Conditions: Slight moon outside, nice summer night. Close to 2 AM.

Investigator Commentary by Marc DeWerth: A telephone and an onsite interview were done. No issues of credibility. There was a remnant of the handprint that had been cleaned but not totally erased. This print was 8'6" from the ground level. The top of the window where the figure was observed was 9 feet from the ground. There was an evident line of travel from the hollow behind the house to the window. It also appeared that something had attempted to pull apart the dog run on the property, leaving a three-inch gap where most of the pressure was applied. A two-inch galvanized steel post was buckled as a result. The witness is adamant that it was not there when put together. The witnesses had contacted the sheriff's office who had dispatched a deputy to the property. The deputy took fingerprints from what remained on the windows after they were cleaned, and from another window where they had not noticed the prints and therefore not cleaned. The witness said the deputy was of the opinion they were not human. Two game cameras were set up but have not acquired any suspicious pictures.

Afterthoughts: I talked to Investigator Marc DeWerth, and he told me when standing at the top of the hollow, it was the most spooked he had ever been. He had a very bad feeling. Ironically for me that hollow leads to where I had one of my own Bigfoot encounters where I had been screamed at and witnessed a tree being shook for around twenty seconds. The family lives within sight of some of my own family, and I think about it each time I'm in the area. Bigfoot appear curious about humans, and it's very common to hear of them looking in the window. I'm personally curious if the other window that had prints on it was the room the girls were in. Bigfoot also naturally seem attracted to children.

Year: 2011
Season: Summer
Month: August
State: Ohio
County: Hocking
Nearest Town: Ewing

Observed: On August 29th I was outside close to dusk with my litter of puppies going potty. I heard the whistle I do to call the adult dogs, a bob white whistle. Thinking it was my parrot in the house I did a few back-and-forth whistles. One of my adult dogs made a deep woof when we heard a loud rustle in the forest. I looked up and saw a tall hairy creature staring at me. It was very dark and let the branch go that it was holding down with its arm and stepped back into the trees. I watched for a while and then my roommate came out the door and we heard a bunch of trees being moved. I asked her if the parrot had been whistling with me and she said no, it had been quiet and eating. We live on the edge of the Hocking Hills and hear knocking and banging a lot, but this is our only sighting.

Conditions: Dusk, just before the sun set.

Investigator Commentary by Dr. Russ Jones: I talked to the witness at length. She has a history of being outdoors and is originally from Minnesota. She used to deer hunt in the past and is comfortable in the outdoors. In addition, I can add the following: the house that she is living in was empty for about one year. They had been inhabiting the house for about six weeks at the time of the incident. The area is typical of the Hocking Hills region, fields backing up to considerable areas of forest. The dog with her was an Australian shepherd, which alerted when she was outside, which was what made her look up. She estimates the branch to be eight to nine feet long and six inches in diameter. They have a pen out back that they take the puppies to occasionally and have dog food and peanut butter for training out there. They have noticed the gate being untied and a musky odor there before.

The Hocking Hills region of Ohio has been an up-and-coming area for sightings. If there is a Bigfoot in the area, it could have been in the woods surrounding the vacant house. The whole area is loaded with deer. I'm sure that a Bigfoot's curiosity would be heightened by a new woman living in a previously unoccupied house and a litter full of whippet puppies.

Afterthoughts: There are seven state parks near this location, and one is the busiest in the country, Old Man's Cave State Park. Hundreds of thousands come each year and walk the trails, camp, and picnic. The parks all close at night, and trail walking only is allowed and only during the day. This leaves a lot of area for resident Bigfoot and predictable patterns of humans. The surrounding areas have a lot of fields but rocky steep hillsides above them that can't be farmed. This case was almost a perfect storm for a Bigfoot sighting.

~

Year: 2011
Season: Winter

Month: February
State: Ohio
County: Gallia
Nearest Town: Cheshire

Observed: I was traveling on Little Kyger Road toward Ohio State Route 7 when I popped over a steep hill located on this stretch of road and as my headlights shown back down on the road as I topped the hill, alongside the road there is a tree and a road sign, that's when I noticed this large very dark figure along the road with what appeared to be either very dark brown or black fur. It was a head taller than the road sign it was walking in front of (6-7 feet tall). It looked as if it was getting ready to cross the road out of a very wet swampy marsh area into more wooded hills. As my lights hit it as without thinking it turned back the way it had come very swiftly. Another interesting thing I noticed as it turned back into the swampy area is that I could see the entire bottom of its foot which was very, very large and light in contrast to the rest of the creature and void of any fur. It put you in the mind of a human foot only very much larger. Just within a flash it was gone. I did stop the following day to see if I could see and kind of tracks and saw nothing but the compaction of the ground and wouldn't yield a footprint as the marshy area, but I didn't leave the road. Very Strange indeed.

Investigator Commentary by Dr. Russ Jones: I talked at length to this witness, who works in the medical community. He is a hunter and often found in the woods. In addition, I can add the closest he was to the animal was around 150 feet. The sighting was at night, but he passes by the sign where the animal was each day and believes the sign to be seven feet high. The animal's head and neck were above the sign. He saw the animal for about five seconds and believes it was headed to a grove of pine trees. Of further interest to me is the fact that the sighting is roughly one mile from the Ohio River. There is a major power plant on the river near the location. Looking at a map of the area, you notice dozens of power line right-of-ways.

Many investigators believe that these may serve as pathways for Bigfoot. Another interesting note is that many people in Ohio call Bigfoot "grassman". The first grassman sightings published in Ohio were in the 1860s and in the same county as this report.

Afterthoughts: How can I give reports and not include a road crossing? It's the most common type of Bigfoot sighting, and in some states, like Georgia, most of the sightings recorded are road sightings. Many Bigfoot researchers are running cameras like GoPros in their vehicles, hoping to just get lucky with a road crossing. One of my friends recently believes he just had one, but it wasn't quite close enough to see clearly.

~

Year: 2001
Season: Fall
Month: December
State: Ohio
County: Ross
Nearest Town: Frankfort

Observed: The last day of deer hunting found me on Route 35 going east out of Dayton, Ohio at 4:30 AM. I was about to go over a bridge at mile marker 29. There was a semi-truck west bound flicking his lights up and down quickly. I had already put my lights on low beam as I reached the bridge in the left lane and slowed down to about 30 mph. I looked over to see what made the semi driver flash his lights up and down so much. To my surprise, I saw a large ape looking animal standing in the west bound land in front of the slowing semi. In the lights of the semi, I saw the animal step off the west bound lane and in three more steps was up and on the brim of the east bound lane. It had to walk past a "No U Turn" sign and the sign was about 8 feet high. The top of its head was even with the sign. I had 3-4 seconds to observe this creature right in front of me to my left. It was facing me the whole time. What I saw gave me goose bumps up and down my back. The hair on the back of my neck and head stood up. As the animal quickly took one more step to its left into the left lane, I knew that what I had just seen was a Bigfoot for sure. About 8 foot tall and long hair from top to bottom (reddish brown). It had a large head with reddish brown glowing eyes. It looked like it had no neck at all. I had to speed up and swerve to the right to miss it. I heard a clunk and went on. I noticed my left side view mirror was folded up against my car. I looked for hair and signs of blood later and found none. I went hunting and killed an 8-point buck only 3 miles from the Bigfoot incident. I will honestly never, ever forget what I saw. I have hunted bear both in Maine (where I was reared), and Montana back in the 60's and 70's. This wasn't any bear that I saw. A bear would not have shook me up like that. No way Possible.

Conditions: 4:30AM. Clear sky, 38 degrees.

Investigator Commentary by Dr. Russ Jones: I interviewed this witness and found him bright, forthright, and honest. He has no reason to be dishonest and had no opinion of Bigfoot previously. He went so far as to call an area trucking company to see if he could hook up with the semi driver but wasn't able to find which company it was. This is a major highway through this portion of the state and surprisingly the first report I have taken on this road. I suspect many are like the truck driver and just drive on. Like so many witnesses who previously never gave a thought to Bigfoot, this gentleman thinks of it commonly and calls me from time to time to talk about it.

Afterthoughts: I can think of three cases where there were multiple cars having a Bigfoot sighting who stopped and exchanged information. I was able to talk to multiple witnesses, and it made the cases compelling. This summer of 2021 there was one in the Babcock State Park area of West Virginia where two witnesses, in different cars and not knowing each other, saw an orangish-colored juvenile Bigfoot run across a two-lane road.

~

Year: 2015
Season: Fall
Month: November
State: Ohio
County: Nicholas
Nearest Town: Summersville

Observed: On November 24th 2015, I was hunting deer during the firearm season back on the hill behind my house. I am going "bonkers" for lack of a better word, trying to process what I saw that day. I was walking up an old dirt road, the ground was wet, leaves, etc. so I was very quiet. I reached an area where I was looking down into the forest. I raised my binoculars because I, at that moment, was expecting to see a smaller black bear. As I was looking at its back, I noticed a very thin white hair line running down the middle of its back. I thought that was a strange marking for a black bear. I continued to watch this "creature" for quite a few moments. I wanted to see its face, slowly it turned its head and as if it were looking into my eyes through the binoculars. Its face was the solid black of the blackest night, very shiny, looked almost like a black leather stretched tight. Its nose was very wide and had huge nostrils. It seemed to be hunkered down by an old fallen tree and it was in the sunshine that was beaming through parts of the forest. It had no hair on the face, everything was black, and its face looked human. I could see ears like mine only black. Its hair on the body was lighter black than on its face and was somewhat thin (compared to black bears hair) and it wasn't dirty or mangled, it looked clean. In the meantime, as I was steadily watching it, small sandstone rocks were coming down by me and the road above, I didn't want to turn and look. I was watching the creature below me and figured it was chipmunks running around behind me causing small rocks to fall, but after seeing that face, I had to look. I saw nothing behind me, when I returned to using the binoculars and looking for it, it was gone, no sound whatsoever. I now feel that something behind trying to get my attention so it could get away. Someone said that it was probably a man in one of those strange looking suits to hunt in. My reply was "he needs to get mental help immediately for the fact that everyone on this mountain this week are carrying high-powered rifles". I never once felt scared or threatened, all was calm. I saw no arms, legs, limbs, I was focused on its head. It wasn't huge, like the width of it, as I stated before, from behind it looked like a small bear (except it had a human like face). I would appreciate any feedback. I forgot to mention that in October and in part of November during bow season I heard some very strange sounds during 3 of my hunting days up there, I call them "jungle sounds", ooh ooh ooh aah aah aah woooo (repeated at a fast pace).

Landscape: forest, dirt road that goes to satellite towers or cellular towers.

Investigator Commentary by Dr. Russ Jones: I have communicated with the witness several times and am very familiar with the area personally. I can confirm this is a reliable report and a believable witness. In addition, the witness was between fifty-five and sixty-five yards from the creature. The sighting lasted between twelve and fifteen minutes. She wouldn't look away from the creature until she saw it and was whispering, "What is it? What is it?" and she believes it may have heard her. When she looked at the face, she noticed the hairline started back farther than a human's would. Upon the return home of her husband, he went back up on top of the hill and found six locust trees twisted off. One top remained, but the other tops of the remaining locust trees were gone. It takes an unbelievable amount of strength to twist a tree several inches in diameter, not to mention locust trees. Is this possible that a nest was being made somewhere in the vicinity? On a side note, investigators talk often about "never take your eyes off the Bigfoot". There are many stories across the country of a witness seeing a Bigfoot only to be distracted by vocals, stick breaking, and/or rock throwing, and when they turn back, the Bigfoot is gone.

Afterthoughts: This witness went on to do some habituation attempts and was having some success. She is one of four hunters whom I have interviewed who had a clear shot and could have shot a Bigfoot.

Year: 2014
Season: Fall
Month: September
State: West Virginia
County: Greenbrier
Nearest Town: Quinwood

Observed: On my way to work this evening, at 8:46 PM. I was driving down the mountain when I saw what I thought was a bear. I slowed down just in case it ran out in front of me. When it stepped over the guardrail, I knew it wasn't a bear. I rolled my window up. It turned, looked at me, had my bright lights on. In two steps it crossed the two-lane road, then went up the mountain. Scared, omg, can't believe what I saw, still shook up! Very dark, that animal was dark, matted hair, from what I could see in my headlights. My guess, height wise, close to nine feet. Very tall. It happened on Carl Mountain near Quinwood, West Virginia.

Investigator Commentary by Dr. Russ Jones: I talked to the witness about her sighting that happened on her way to work and can add the following. While driving down the mountain at about 40 mph, she saw a deer jump the guardrail and run across the road and keep looking back across the road. She slowed almost to a stop, anticipating another deer to cross. The Bigfoot stepped over the guardrail about thirty feet in front of her and looked at her stopped vehicle. She started honking her horn and flashing her lights to try to scare it. She was shaking as soon as she saw the Bigfoot. She noticed dark reddish-brown hair, large eyes, which reflected an orangish color. She was struck by the size; her brother is six feet seven and a big guy but would be dwarfed by this animal. The Bigfoot did not seem aggressive. The nearest house was about a mile away. She sees all types of animals on the road, including bears, and it was not anything like that. When she got to work, she told the other workers what she had seen and was later approached by a woman whose father was a coal miner and had seen a Bigfoot in the middle of the night close to the same location. She gets very anxious when thinking about the sighting. Now before bed she makes sure all the outside lights are on and her dogs are inside.

As always, I try to figure out why a Bigfoot would be at the location of the sighting. It is very remote with a lot of terrain similar to everywhere in West Virginia. There are a great deal of power line right-of-ways in that area, making travel easy and creating edge for deer. It is a hardwood forest at about 2,600 feet elevation. Greenbrier County is one of the most common counties for Bigfoot sightings in West Virginia. It is a prime location, and I took *Finding Bigfoot* there for an episode of the show.

Afterthoughts: There's not that many places that you can be a mile from a house, but Appalachia has places that are many miles from the nearest house. I'm always amazed and find it interesting that in most cases you can spend hundreds of hours in the woods and not hear much, and the resident Bigfoot population just seems to move away from you. Other times they will walk right out in front of people or a car. It's the exception rather than the rule, but it happens. Just like tracks, you may find one or two a few times a year, but on occasion there will be trackway. I guess like people, Bigfoot individually behave differently.

~

Year: 2007
Season: Winter
Month: November
State: West Virginia
County: Fayette
Nearest Town: Fayetteville

Observed: To keep it short. I was deer hunting in the New River Gorge in Fayetteville, WV and it was 2007, the week of Thanksgiving. It was evening with about two hours of daylight left and I noticed movement about 60 yards towards the gorge from my position. I raised the gun to view the movement through the scope. After holding it in position for 10 seconds or so, I saw a very large hand appear from the side of a large poplar tree. It was palm against the tree, and I saw fingers mostly. Then to my surprise I saw a head peek from around the large tree and two LARGE eyes affixed on a head of a creature I had never seen before. I'm a hunter and have been since I'm 8, I'm now 38. The Bigfoot blinked twice while looking at me and then stepped back behind the tree. I viewed it for about 20 seconds while it was looking at me. My mind just couldn't figure out what it was, and I knew what it wasn't. I had no desire to shoot it and very well could have but my mind and body almost seemed to be in a state of shock while viewing it. I had the cross near the location on the trail to get out of the woods and I was F'n terrified even with a loaded deer rifle. My hair stood on end when I realized that I would have to go towards the location to get out of the woods. I called my uncle as soon as I got to my jeep and told him, he believed me. I am a VERY honest man and would never lie about this. The thing is though, I never heard it run away or move through the leaves. You can hear movement from 200+ yards off in these woods. It's like it just disappeared. I came home very shaken from the experience, and it changed my life. Now I know what is out there. It was very cool looking, about 7 feet tall, it had very large dark pupils. Around the pupils, its eyes were almost owl like. It had brownish-blonde fur and it had a visible face. It almost looked like the troll faces that you used to put on your pencil as kids, really. It was very clean looking and not what you would expect. Its fingers were long and thick with no fur, and it hard dark fingernails. I had my scope on 9 power and it was equivalent to being about 30 feet from me visually. It was real and I would take a polygraph and swear on my life.

Landscape: Top of river gorge in mixed mesophytic forest.

Investigator Commentary by Dr. Russ Jones: I interviewed the witness, who has multiple degrees from WVU. He is a thirty-nine-year-old avid outdoorsman. I hiked to the area of the sighting and was able to see the New River Gorge Bridge. One thing I found interesting was the power line right-of-way literally at the location of the sighting. The gorge area itself is very steep with rough terrain.

Afterthoughts: Twenty-something-odd years ago a troubled man parked on the New River Gorge Bridge and jumped to his death. His car was parked right where he jumped, yet dog crews and searchers never found his body. It was found twenty years later by some rock climbers. This bridge is one of the most recognized features on the east coast but is inhospitable below it. There are few trails, and the gorge itself is rocky, snaky, and can be almost too steep to climb. I've spent hundreds and hundreds of hours in the gorge and had several Bigfoot encounters among the two hundred ghost towns scattered on the steep gorge mountainsides. I always take pictures to try to show how steep it is, and they just don't do it justice. It can take an hour and a half for a fit person to climb out of the gorge itself.

Year: 1961
Season: Summer
Month: June

State: West Virginia
County: Wayne
Nearest Town: Huntington

Observed: I am a 65-year-old physician living in Ocala, Florida. I grew up in Huntington, West Virginia. When I was 14 years old, I was with my best friend Bill, also 14 years old, and we were walking in the woods behind my grandparents' dairy farm. We had a .22 rifle with us, and we had been roaming around for about an hour when we came to a clearing at the top of the hill. We suddenly saw an animal neither of us recognized. When we first saw it, it was bent over doing something with its upper extremities. We were mesmerized for several minutes and didn't move. It then seemed to become aware of us. What happened next freaked us out. It stood up on its back legs and looked right at us. We were terrified. It was very tall, blackish colored hair, also skinny in appearance with a tapered face. It was standing at the edge of a pine thicket. It turned away from us and jumped over a barbed wire fence. Even though we had a gun we ran as fast as we could back to the farmhouse to relay the story to my grandfather. I know this description is somewhat different from what you've probably heard, but we saw an animal I've never seen before or since. S******** P***** M.D.

Investigator Commentary by Dr. Russ Jones: I have communicated with this physician living in Florida a number of times. Although the report is older, it's still important in historical terms. There are still sightings in the area the sighting took effect, so this reinforces the BFRO belief in the halibut effect, essentially, that as long as conditions are similar, there is a good chance of finding similar animals in the same place they have shown up historically. In addition to what the witness said in the report, he also added that it was a "frightening experience" not because the animal was threatening in any way, but that it was an unknown animal that was seen. Without any question it was tall, black, and bipedal. To this day he will not enter the woods without being armed.

I have met with hundreds of witnesses, and it's very common to hear that the sighting was a "life-altering" experience. It's very common to hear that the witness will think of the experience commonly through their lifetime.

Afterthoughts: I often wonder whether it's more the outdoor people who struggle with the sighting and think of it so much because it was a life-changing and "belief system" change. Being in the woods all the time, we form a belief system of the things in the woods, and for something to change all that causes a disruption. I think of my experiences each day, but that may because I'm so intimately involved in the field. I've had others such as a teacher and welder who have said they think of it almost daily. One witness had given me a photo he had drawn. I told him I would get it back to him, and he told me he had hundreds and to keep it.

Year: 2007
Season: Summer
Month: July
State: Tennessee
County: Gibson
Nearest Town: Kenton

Observed: This happened on my grandparent's farm which they still live on, and I still visit almost weekly. I was probably 12 at the time and it was summer so my grandparents would allow my sister (10 at the time) and I to have sleepovers at their house. There were probably 7 of us staying over that night and we had been outside all day and were from all over the area. For a little background on the location of the sighting, my grandparent's house is situated between two small towns with populations of 1000 each. The farm is also about 10 minutes from 3 different wildlife areas. They had no neighbors at the time other than cows and corn. Now they have one neighbor whose house you can see from the yard but no other visible neighbors. Around 11PM we decided to go outside because we were being loud, and my grandparents had gone to bed. We had done this probably a half dozen times over the summer. We had been outside for probably 30 minutes to an hour when we started to hear odd noises in the cornfield across the road and the sound of corn stalks breaking. This continued probably over the next 20-30 minutes. As a bunch of 10–12-year-old girls we ignored the sounds and kept talking all the while my grandparent's 3 dogs were sitting in front of us with tails tucked growling like something was in the cornfield that was maybe 50 yards from where we were sitting in my grandparent's front yard. We heard a loud scream from the cornfield as something came out of the field right in front of us. What came out of the field was a tall humanoid creature covered in dark brown hair that was slightly taller than the corn was at the time at about 6-7 feet. We all looked at the creature and took off running back towards the house leaving all of our things outside. Once we got inside, we looked at each other in utter shock at what we had seen. None of us wanted to say anything to my grandparents because we all thought they would call us crazy. Of the seven of us that saw the creature, 4 of us had been raised hunting and fishing. We knew the animals native to the area and spent hours in the woods with our fathers and grandfathers learning how to track animals and respect nature. To this day I am afraid to be outside at their house at night by myself. I have heard the same noises again and again over the years including screams and wood knocks.

Conditions: Around midnight. Clear night. A dusk to dawn light was in the area throwing off light.

Investigator Commentary by Dr. Russ Jones: Is the report less believable because it's several young girls? Does it matter that there have been several other reports within a couple of miles of the sighting? Does it make it compelling that the witness filed a report twelve years later? It still stuck with her. Is it more intriguing that all the girls agree on what happened? The area is exactly the type of area where you would expect a Bigfoot might be.

Afterthoughts: The biggest thing in common that Bigfoot witnesses have is that they had a Bigfoot sighting. Other than that, they are woodsmen, people who have never been in the woods (since a road sighting is most common), all ages, and all occupations. They have nothing else in commonality that would tend to produce an increased likelihood of a Bigfoot sighting. Bigfoot witnesses are geographic not demographic.

Year: 2006
Season: Winter
Month: December
State: Kentucky
County: Harlan
Nearest Town: Harlan

Observed: It was the opening morning of Kentucky black powder deer hunt. I had found a saddle on a map that was almost 3 miles back into the hills. I went into the saddle two days before and found a big rock overlooking a draw and the ridge that leads into the saddle. It was somewhere around 1 hour before daylight that I was slipping up the ridge about a quarter mile from the rock. All at once something jumped up out of the tall grass on my left side. I turned on my 2 AA flashlight and turned it toward whatever had jumped up. 2 sets of red/orange eyes were looking at me no more than 50 yards away. The bigger of the 2 looked to be around 7 feet tall and the other about 2 feet smaller. With my small light I could not see for sure what I was looking at. All I could see was 2 dark things looking at me. All at once they took off running and their eyes disappeared. I spotted the eyes again going out the ridgeline about 100 yards in front of me. I thought it was bears standing up looking at me, so I didn't think much of it. I got to the rock and set up my gear for the hunt. I wear scent lock clothes when I deer hunt and I also drag a rag with deer pee on it behind me to mask my scent. I tied my orange vest up in a limb over my head so other hunters could see me. I put my ghillie suit on and set back and waited for daylight. Right at the break of daylight I was looking into the saddle for a buck. All at once a stick about 2 foot long came flying at me and landed right behind me. I turned and looked and seen this big black brown monkey looking thing squatted looking at me about 50 yards away. My first thought was somebody was teasing me or trying to run me off. I stand up and yelled HEY YOU BETTER SAY SOME- THING OR I WILL SHOOT. I pointed my black powder, and it moved its arm back and I could see it had another stick in its hands. I yelled again, all at once it came rushing at me. I shot in front of it, and it turned and took off. It went about 75 yards and stopped. It stood up and looked over toward a thicket and grunted. A smaller one came running out making a crying sound. By this time, I had already reloaded and was headed off the rock away from the things. I walked out and left all my gear. The next day I went back in to get my gear. When I got there my backpack was tore open and my things were laying everywhere. I had crackers and potted meat and some coke colas. The cans had been hit on a rock and busted open. Anything that was food ate. I had a knife and a game boy in my pack also. They were still there, that proves it was not somebody as they would have taken them. The limb my vest was on was broken out. My drag line was gone. I think I seen a mom and a baby Bigfoot. Where I had scent lock clothes and had deer pee on a drag rag they could not smell that I was human. I also had a ghillie suit on. I think it thought I was one of them.

Conditions: Early morning, light rain.

Investigator Commentary by Jack Smarr: I followed up with a tele- phone interview to the witness and have this to add: The witness was wearing a ghillie suit, rubber boots, and scent-lock clothes while carrying a rag with deer urine on it. The grass was waist to chest deep in the reclaimed mine area where he first encountered the two Squatches. In the dark, using a small flashlight, he thought he had jumped two bears and continued on to his hunting spot. It was only in the early daylight, when he turned his body in reaction to a stick being thrown at him, he realized that he was looking at something that was not a bear. Although it looked like an ape, he thought someone was pulling a prank on him. The Sasquatch had another stick in its hand and looked like it was winding up for another toss when he yelled the second time. The crouching figure went into a "football stance" and started down after him. The hunter fired a shot in self-defense. He did not aim at the creature, but in front as a deterrent. The Sasquatch immediately stopped the charge and retreated up the hill and away from him, where it came to a halt. The creature grunted as a possible signal, whereupon the smaller one came out of hiding to meet back up with the larger one. The grunt was low, powerful, and guttural. The small one wailed as it ran, in a high-pitched "half woman scream and half baby crying" manner. Once the two connected back up, they left the scene. Being in an open grassy area, the hunter did not hear them move, nor did they leave tracks.

I believe that the witness had two interactions with the Sasquatches. The first one was in the tall grass on the way to the hunting spot, and the second one at the hunting spot. I believe that the Sasquatches were confused by the ghillie suit and the lack of human scent. I also believe the Sasquatches were checking him out on the boulder and threw a stick at him to see what he would do. The hunter witnessed a charge and communication between two Sasquatches. One would assume it was a false charge, but since it was broken up by the firing of his rifle, I cannot say. It was not bears; bears don't throw sticks. The Sasquatches did not yell or scream at him. They did not knock on wood, nor did they clap their hands. The only communication was when the large one wanted the small one to come up to where it was so they could leave together.

Afterthoughts: I've heard a couple of these kinds of cases, and while the Bigfoot didn't attack, it always makes me think I want a firearm with me in the woods. The odds of a case similar are low because most aren't going so far in the woods and also wearing a ghillie suit. I think clearly the Bigfoot did not know what the hunter was. Bluff charges do happen, commonly at night; investigator Brad Kennan experienced one in Ohio. "Imagine a freight train coming through the woods." I'm sure that if there are real charges, we probably don't know, as the witness would be gone.

～

Year: 2019
Season: Spring
Month: April
State: Virginia
County: Wythe
Nearest Town: Wytheville

Observed: My wife and I were driving around, and we were on a back road out in Wytheville, Virginia on Queens knob Road. It was dark out, not too late, but it was dark and as we turned a corner my wife and I saw something in the middle of the road. It was about 4 feet tall and covered in fur. It was NOT a dog or any 4-legged animal. It was on 2 legs, and it saw our car and ran and jumped over a fence towards the left like it was nothing. It pumped its arms it ran then jumped over the fence without using any effort at all. It then proceeded to run through the field with the sheep and we lost sight of it. My wife and I both talked about what we saw, and we both had no doubts in our minds.

Investigator Commentary by Charles Kimbrough: I spoke with the witness within a week of the incident. The witness was driving home after fishing. It was just getting dark. The time was between 7:30 p.m. and 8 p.m.; Johnathon and his wife saw what they described as a monkey-looking animal about four feet tall with very long arms. It was blackish brown in color. He said it ran in front of his vehicle and jumped a ditch and fence with ease. After it jumped in the air, it grabbed the fence with one hand and propelled itself over onto the other side. It then ran through a small field where sheep are being kept. After looking on a map, I noticed it was running towards a thin patch of trees it could use as cover to continue to a larger forested area. The witness said that even though it was so small, its steps were much longer than his. The witness claims this isn't the first time they've seen this thing. Sometime last year, they saw it run across the road within a hundred feet of this crossing, but this is the first time they've reported it to the BFRO. The witness sounded very sincere. His wife was even commenting in the background of the phone conversation, and she sounded a bit shaken over the incident. He couldn't understand why it was so small, when every Bigfoot story he's ever heard says that Bigfoot are over eight feet tall. So I don't believe that if they were going to make up a story, it would be of a four-foot-tall Bigfoot.

Afterthoughts: Bigfoot is a species, so they have infants, young, middle-aged, and old. It's fairly common to hear of a Bigfoot that a witness believes might have had a younger one with it. I suspect that the greatest number of reports are of adolescent or young adult Bigfoot looking for new territory or even a mate.

Year: 1991
Season: Winter
Month: February
State: Pennsylvania
County: Berks
Nearest Location: On Appalachia Trail, State Game Land 110.
Marshall's path.

Observed: The sighting was in 1991 in Blue Mountain, Berks County PA. State Game Land 110. I believe early February. I was grouse hunting on the top of the mountain, there was ten to twelve inches of snow with a half to one inch of ice on top of the snow. It was very difficult to puncture your feet to walk through the snow and ice. I shot my grouse, on top of the mountain about a 1/2 to 3/4 of a mile from where we came up to the top of the mountain. I shot twice after my friend, and I yelled grouse. I yelled I got it to my friend who then proceeded to walk to me. He was 75 yards away and it took him about 15-20 minutes to get up to me. Then he walked a trail that went back to where the road starts at the top of the mountain. I stood there for 15 minutes as I heard my friend walking away from me, after I could no longer hear his footsteps, I turned the other direction and was looking at the side of the mountain that we came up. I noticed a dark figure running along the ridge of the top of the mountain for 50 to 100 yards. It ran, there was an opening and it stopped. Then it proceeded to run straight for me uphill and did not stop until it was about 40 to 50 feet away from me. It was not out of breath and did not make a sound it just stood there and looked at me for 1-2 minutes, and then walked away in the direction it had come from. First of all, in those conditions you could not run or barely walk in it. It was hard to puncture the ice on top of the snow to walk let alone run. It went through like it wasn't even there for 200 yards and when it stopped 50 feet away, you couldn't even see it or hear it breathe. He ran that distance, in about 1-3 minutes maybe. It scared the hell out of me, I wasn't sure what it was until it stopped right in front of me. It found me; I wasn't looking for it. And I can tell that when he stopped in the opening on the ridge that he can see blaze orange because he ran faster than straight for me after he seen me in my blaze orange one-piece outfit. He was there in no time at all, running uphill 100 to 150 yards. He walked away and looked back at me once and then kept going. He was all black, very long hair, it was hard to see his face through all of the hair. Tall, around 7 to 7 1/2, 400-500 pounds I thought. Very powerful animal seemed very intelligent because I think he heard the gunshots or the yelling and wanted to find who was making the noise on the mountain and came right at me. I was scared at first when it stopped. I put my shotgun right on it at 45-50 feet and it didn't even flinch, it wasn't scared, it just walked away. My friend with me is 6'1" 200 pounds and when I told him what happened, he didn't believe me, but he tried to run on the road at the top of the mountain on level ground, flat, he took 3 steps and fell on his face.

Conditions: Close to noon, lighting conditions were overcast.

Landscape: Top of mountain, wooded area.

Investigator Commentary by Jim Osborne: When I spoke to the witness, he stated that it looked like the creature in the Patterson film. He added that as it was walking away, it turned to look at him by turning its upper torso, not just the head. Witness emphasized that the creature's actions in the snow was an unbelievable display of power to move so swiftly and effortlessly on difficult terrain. He also stated that once the creature spotted him and moved toward him, he felt that he was about to die (he had only light shot in the gun, and there was no way he could run away in the snow at the speed the creature was approaching). However, once the creature stopped and displayed no aggression, then he no longer felt threatened. When asked to better describe the face, he said that there was so much hair, and the eyes were so deep-set, it was like looking at a mask—impossible to determine whether the features under the hair were more human or apelike.

Afterthoughts: It's so hard to know what was going on in this case with the Bigfoot behavior. My guess is that they are familiar with humans hunting and what the sounds are that are associated with it and was going to try to steal some game that had been shot. There are hundreds of cases where witnesses were led to believe by Bigfoot behavior that they know what guns are and are leery of them.

~

Year: 2017
Season: Fall
Month: October
State: Virginia
County: Page
Nearest Town: Stanley

Observed: I was bush hogging my lower field on my farm and for some reason I cannot remember I stopped and got off of my ATV. I had a look onto the top side of my neighbor's property and saw a large black object which initially looked like a large Black Angus bull laying down. I said to myself that he doesn't have any cows at all. Then I thought it might have been one of mine that escaped. I focused a little closer. Its head was rather strange because I really could not distinguish a head. It seem to turn it body slightly towards me then it happened. It took off in the strangest way I have ever seen. It sprung and it was not a bear, these incredibly long arms came out and it did not run but threw its arms out in front and swung its legs almost in front of its arms then sprung forward again. I measured the distance it covered on Google Earth and it's roughly 80 yards. It covered this distance in three leaps which I distinctly remember. While it leapt, I saw how long it was, not bulky like a bear but extremely long. I kept staring in awe, like did I really see that, then it leapt back over the hill as if to see if I was still looking at it, then went back over the hill and was gone. I ran to get my binos, but it was gone for good.

Conditions: 5:30 PM, bright warm sunny day.

Investigator Commentary by Charles Kimbrough: I spoke to the witness over the phone. He claims that while he was bush hogging his field, he saw something dark and large and looked as though it were lying down on his neighbor's property. He said he stopped to look because he thought it might be one of his cows that got out. His neighbor doesn't have any cows. But as he was watching it, it stood up and proved to be much larger than he thought and was standing upright. It then took three very large hops away from him. He could see its arms swinging as it leapt. It cleared a very large distance with three leaps. After going over the hill, it came back and looked down at him, then left again. He said that he would have gone over and looked for prints, but he doesn't have a good relationship with the owner of the bordering land. Although it was a great distance away from him, he is 100% sure of what he saw. This property is only one and a half miles away from the Shenandoah National Park and the Appalachian Trail. There have been sightings in the park in the past.

Afterthoughts: I put this report in for two reasons. First, the report, like many I am using, has not been made public because of the witness. In the past I have had mayors, defense contractors, and other well-known public figures who have had sightings but desire to be kept private. It's important enough for them that they are willing to take the chance that someone may hear about it because it was important to them. Clearly no reason to hoax a report or take a chance having their name out there. This lends credence to the report. Secondly, it sounds as if when the animal jumped up, it started moving on all fours before it ran upright. Bigfoot does not only move on two legs; it's common to see it move on four or even do both in the same sighting.

Year: 2005
Season: Summer
Month: June
State: Tennessee
County: Cumberland
Nearest Town: Crossville

Observed: I live in a retirement community known as xxxxxxxx xxxxxxx in East Tennessee. Knoxville is the nearest large city and is 65 miles east. Our little community is surrounded on almost three sides by a State Forest and the Catoosa Wildlife Refuge. We have an overabundance of "protected" wildlife of all kinds (including too many deer, in my opinion) that venture, at will, into our community. Always the bold tomboy, I preferred to get my exercise by hiking the heavily forested back roads and trails near our home instead of playing golf as my husband did. I never hiked more than 6 miles from home, and always in the early morning. One morning, I was approximately 4 miles from my home when I came upon an unexpected sunny clearing that seemed to be an old road or path at one time because it brushy and void of undergrowth and trees. On my hikes I am normally under a canopy of very tall trees. So, the sunlight was an unexpected pleasure. As I rounded a curve and my eyes caught the filtered sunlight from the clearing, I observed a large ape-like creature jump from the woods and pounce on something on the ground. I abruptly froze. In a flash, the creature stood back up holding a long snake by the head. Just s quick as this happened, the creature disappeared back into the cover of the woods alongside the clearing. I remained still for a moment contemplating whether the animal had seen me and how best to protect myself. I literally heard my heart beating. I quickly ruled out tree climbing and decided the only alternative was to turn in the opposite direction and run as fast as my legs would carry me. I ran nearly all the way home. I was so disturbed by what I had seen, I decided that no one would believe it, so I never told anyone. That was about 5-6 years ago, and my husband has since died. Over the years, I have tried to convince myself that I really didn't see the thing that had so frightened me that morning in the woods. I tried to convince myself that I had somehow imagined it; however, the vivid memory persists. To this day, I have never set foot in any woods again, essentially breaking a very longstanding and much revered habit that day, I am still fearful of seeing that creature again. I have always been a sober-minded individual, not at all given to making up fantasies or stretching the truth as I know it. I was completely caught off guard and stunned the other day when an ad spot for your show came across my TV screen. After watching the show, I am now convinced that I actually did see what I thought I saw that day on my last hike. Your show also brought to mind the night a few years ago. This happened well after my experience in the woods. My husband and I were sitting on our deck looking up at the stars, so clearly visible up her on a clear night in the dark woods of the Cumberland Plateau. We were quietly listening for the Whippoorwill who nests every year in the woods across our street. He calls relentlessly for a mate ever night during season. Piercing through the peace and tranquility we heard the most horrific deep bellowing scream from what seemed like some distance away. We had both been leaning way back in our lawn chairs admiring the night sky, and almost fell out of our chairs in shock. I remember my husband abruptly stood up and said we should go inside, and he added that he had never seen a mountain lion big enough to scream like that. I did not make the mental connection to the scream we heard and the creature that I had seen a few years prior until I saw your show and heard your team members calling out to Bigfoot. Oh my gosh! That was the same sound! I must confess that I am a reluctant convert!

Conditions: Early morning, sunny, moderately warm.

Investigator Commentary by Dr. Thomas Bruns: I contacted this witness and found her to be very credible. She has a professional business background and is also a professional photographer. I have the following from our conversation: The area where the sighting occurred was on an old trail wide enough for one vehicle. The creature was described as having brown/black hair approximately two to three inches in length, which appeared muddy and unkempt. The head did seem to be larger in the back than the front sloping forehead, and the neck was very short. The one cheek she could see appeared "fat" and the skin a black/charcoal in the sunlight. She only noticed one side of the head. The animal was estimated to be six feet in height and viewed at a distance of one hundred feet. It was very agile as it jumped out and grabbed the snake. The animal appeared "solid" with equal girth between the shoulders, chest, and back. This sighting occurred south of the Catoosa Wildlife Management Area, in middle/north Tennessee. This area has eighty thousand acres of protected land with numerous creeks, gorges, and abundant wildlife. The close proximity to the Fairfield Glade allows these animals to wander freely in this developing community, providing a large population of deer, turkey, and other wild animals. This entire area, overall, has the essentials for providing a prime Sasquatch habitat.

Afterthoughts: Once again a Bigfoot sighting has a long-lasting effect on a witness. I always assumed my accounts always made such an impression on me because of all the time in the woods and outdoors, but it clearly makes an impression on non-hunters as well, as evidenced by the many reports. This witness didn't tell anyone for years out of fear of being made fun of or not believed, and I imagine there are thousands of sightings that have not been reported for similar reasons. In addition, note the Bigfoot being an opportunistic feeder/hunter. There is much food to be had in the woods that humans wouldn't typically think about.

Year: 2010
Season: Summer
Month: June
State: Pennsylvania
County: Forest
Nearest Town: Marienville

Observed: I have debated whether or not to report my encounter to the BFRO or any organization. I don't know why, but I guess I wanted to keep this experience to myself for a few years and then it just didn't seem to matter as far as reporting it. But now, I realize that all encounters need to be in a data base somewhere. These DO exist and when that day of discovery happens, this database will house many of the answers. My encounter happened in early June of 2010. I took a friend to the Marienville/Timberline ATV trails northeast of Marienville, Pennsylvania in the Allegheny National Forest, to ride ATVs for the day. The Allegheny National Forest covers approximately 515,000 acres or 800 square miles of protected wilderness in Northwest Pal. The forest is pretty dense in most spots and has many types of terrain. From my understanding the Allegheny National Forest is one of the least populated areas east of the Mississippi River. Surrounding the forest are more woodlands and farm country. The two trail systems we were riding that weekend join together and make an approximate 60–80-mile loop from the northern end down to the bottom, and then back up to the other side of the loop. My encounter happened on the return trip back up, heading north. I remember it rained very hard the night before and through the early morning because my friend, who was new to ATV'ing, didn't bring rain gear. We had to go buy him some cheap rain gear and then headed up to the trail. It rained the first half hour or so of our ride and I remember the sun coming out and it was turning into a really nice day for a ride. For those that ride ATV's they know that rain makes mud, which is much more fun to ride in than dust. A few hours into the ride, having stopped and observed some beaver dams, some very old oil wells, a couple of logged out area where it seemed like you could see for miles and other cool sites that the forest had to offer. I was getting in more of a hurry to get back, it was approaching the end of the day. My buddy was way behind me, so I decided to stop on the trail and wait for him. I usually don't separate from ATV buddies when riding, but this part of the trail was an abandoned logging trail and pretty easy, so I rode ahead for a while and then decided to stop and wait for him. He didn't ride fast or dangerous, he "putted" so I knew he was safe, just slow. If he didn't show up, I would've turned around and met up with him. I wasn't sitting long; I just took my helmet off. That's when I noticed rocks kept hitting the front right side of my ATV. They weren't large rocks, maybe just about hand sized. It took a minute or so before it occurred to me that I was stopped and that rocks shouldn't be flying through the air and hitting my ATV. I was turning my head toward the right to follow the path of these "air rocks" as I called them when my turn stopped. I noticed this "stump" which turned out to be a dark figure, approximately 70-90 feet away, that appeared to be in a sitting or crouching, or just a low position, then stand up into an upright position. I'll never forget how it seemed to pop right up like it was on a spring, with very little effort. Initially I looked at its hands because I was interested what was in its hand if anything. It was much taller than a normal human, best guess 7.5 feet or so, and absolutely not a bear. It was VERY broad at the shoulders. Almost freakishly broad- I remember that very well. It was on two legs, and I could see its right arm hanging down, which was on the left side because it was facing me. I remember that I wanted to watch its right hand to see if "it" was armed or what it might be doing. That is funny to me now, because for some reason I assumed it was right-handed. It moved its right arm to a slightly bent position, stopping with its hand in front of it, at about its waist. Its left arm stayed hanging to its side-very long arms. It was all very dark black-a shiny black- from head to toe, or as far as I could see to its fee as it was standing in 1-2-feet-tall grass or taller. As my eyes made their way up the creature, I could see that its head was all black as well. There was no white or lighter caller that stood out, like most animals would have on their face. I could not see clear details of the face as it was all black but it did not appear to have hair on its face. It appeared to be black skin-the same color black as the hair but I could tell there wasn't hair in some spots. I noticed the eyes were black, or very dark and deep, with a pronounced brow ridge. I could obviously tell that it had a face. I just couldn't see defined detail of the lips or anything as it was all the same color. The lips were closed and a straight line across the face, not open mouthed, smile or frown, just straight lips. The hair was short to medium length and not shaggy. I'd say the hair was an average of 3-5 inches long, shorter at the head. It was almost groomed in appearance, but I think it's from the hair being short and thick. At least that was my impression. Oddly, I did not notice any mud or dirt all over it, which seemed odd because it had rained hard the night before and didn't stop until several hours before this. The trails were muddy. Almost as soon as my eyes were at its head and face and I was trying to "zoom in" and get a better look at the face, it began to leave. It didn't turn and walk away, but rather it stepped straight back into the brush and trees and not take its eyes away from me. It stayed square to me as it was moving backwards. This all happened in a span of no more than 30 seconds, from the time I noticed the rocks hitting my ATV, up until it moved backwards. When I play it over in my head it seems like 30 minutes. At this point an overwhelming fear just filled my mind, and I remember feeling like I shouldn't be in this spot right now. I don't remember shaking in fear or anything like that, but I felt warm and almost like I was going to puke. So, I hit the gas and took off. I wish now that I wouldn't have just fled, but the feeling that came over me was not like I'd experienced before. I had my smart phone in my fender bag, and it NEVER occurred to me to get it out and start video. I honestly couldn't move for a period of time. I have been surprised by people walking up on me in the woods and hunted all of my life, so animal encounters, even bear from a distance, do not scare, or alarm me. I was in the military for six years and actually had the honor to serve as SEAL TEAM 4 and SDV TEAM 2 support as a special warfare boat crew. During that time, I had many highly anxious experiences, and one would imagine. To summarize, I am pretty observant, I don't have a tendency to overreact, and I don't scare easy. I am very levelheaded and not crazy. I didn't instantly think "Bigfoot" as I wasn't a real believer then. At least I doubted their existence in the Eastern US and if they existed it was only in the Northwest US, Canada, or Alaska. This encounter took my emotions to places where they had not been or at least had not been for a long time. It has been going through my head for over 4 years. I didn't tell anyone except my fiancé within the first year of the encounter. Now, quite a few people know. The person I was riding with that day just found out in 2014. I never told him about the story but because I couldn't remember if it was spring/early summer or late summer/early fall, he naturally ask why, what's up? I told him what happened. It turns out that he believes in these creatures. He then realized why I was acting so weird when we finally caught back up with each other, and then on the 2-and-a-half-hour truck ride home. Now I wish I would have told him then. Maybe we could have joined together and gone back to look for signs or whatever we could find. Instead, the overwhelming feeling of "what in the heck was that", and "I can't tell anyone, they won't believe me anyways" took over, and kept it to myself. Nobody has to tell me what I saw or didn't see. I know what I saw. I saw a large dark figure with hair that could throw rocks (and very accurately), stand within 100 feet from me, in a large dense forest where there aren't any cabins or people just hanging out. I still do leave the option open for an extremely large man (larger than anyone I have ever met) in a heavily padded ghillie suit with hair on it standing about 100 feet from the trail just waiting for someone to stop in that exact spot so he could throw rocks at him and take a chance of getting shot (most folks on ATV's will pack a handgun when riding deep in the woods. At least that's my experience). Now that's being sarcastic but trying to make a truth out of what happened. Of course, that option is still slim, but it will always be there as I didn't walk up to this thing and shake its hand or hug it, so being 100% sure if it was a Sasquatch just isn't possible. I am at 99.99% sure though. I do know this, it was a fear I've never felt for a long time, if ever, took over me for a while. Something told me to go, to move on, that I shouldn't be here right now. Again, I am a rational person.

Investigator Summary by Sybilla Irwin: I have spoken with this witness and have met him personally. I find him 100% credible. These details can be added: There were no trees between him and the Sasquatch to obscure any part of his view. He originally thought it might be leaning forward because the arms were so long. The witness had a camera and a gun, but it never occurred to him to use either. The witness described the eyes as being totally dark, seeing no white in the eyes at all. The creature was very thick chested, three feet wide, and very muscular, weighing approximately five hundred pounds. Its fingers were unusually long, and he saw much muscular definition in the biceps. The hair was shiny black and three to four inches in length.

Afterthoughts: Obviously by training this gentleman is a very good observer. I know this experience has shaped his life after the experience. His points about the odds of someone being there to hoax are well taken. The same can be said of many of the experiences and footprints found. It seems unreasonable that someone would be miles back in a wilderness, hoping to hoax someone when they are in most cases carrying a weapon. It seems unlikely that someone would take the time to make fake footprints when it's unlikely that someone would ever be in the location to find them. Considering the thousands of tracks reported all across North America, it would take a large group of hoaxers to complete the task, going back decades.

~

Year: 2012
Season: Fall
Month: November
State: Tennessee
County: Unicoi
Nearest Town: Erwin

Observed: Observed a giant bi-pedal creature in the Cherokee National Forest in Unicoi County, Tennessee near the North Carolina border. Creature was in the creek when I first saw it. The creature immediately sensed my presence and came out of the creek and placed its hand on a tree and hit the tree in a knocking manner approximately 4 times. I was trying to get my phone out and attempt to take a picture when the creature stomped the ground with its foot and growled something fierce several times. A growl I can best describe as a mix between a bear and a large canine. After the growl I started to retreat and as I did the creature took off in a run and vanished. I was in there very close range of 15 to 20 yards when I observed it. If there had not been running water, I don't believe I would have gotten that close to it as it masked it hearing me and me hearing it. The time of the day was 7 AM and I was in the woods going to go trout fishing. I watched the creature around 45 seconds and height estimate is at least 8 feet and shoulder to shoulder 3 feet as length. The creature had brown and red hair that was very thick, yet had a shine in the coat, a flat face and a distinct, almost white nose that looked very wide, and brown eyes. I am very fortunate to see what I saw and all the details of the creature as I was very close to it. I am a believer in sasquatches and just feel so fortunate to have this experience. I didn't feel threatened by the creature just in awe of its massive size and agility as it leapt out of the creek and how quickly it ran out of sight.

Also Noticed: Distinct unknown odor such as wet dog or animal would smell with a musky aroma

Landscape: Hardwood Forest with laurel thickets along a moderate sized creek near a trailer campground.

Investigator Commentary by Rolf Gehman: I spoke to the witness on three occasions and find him to be a credible witness. At first sight the Bigfoot was in the creek water up to its knees; they made eye contact with each other. It leaped with amazing agility out of the water and onto the bank. Next, the Bigfoot stomped its foot on the ground. The Bigfoot looked at the witness and gave what was described as a moan growl scream. The witness then saw and heard the Bigfoot step toward and strike a tree four times with its hand. It then immediately ran toward and into the thick forest. The hair at the head and shoulder was a lighter tint of reddish brown; the rest of the body was darker.

Afterthoughts: What I was most interested by in this report was the hand striking the tree. Wood knocking is considered to be the most common Bigfoot communication. There is speculation, but no one can say for certain what the knocks or number of knocks may mean. There are only a couple of reports in North America where someone saw a Bigfoot making the sound. It's been speculated that it can be cause by a Bigfoot striking a tree, as in this case, a mouth pop, or a hand clap. I believe it's clear here that there must have been other Bigfoot in the area, as evidenced by the Bigfoot knocking.

Year: 2003-2004
Season: Summer
Month: July
State: Kentucky
County: Lawrence
Nearest Town: Blaine

Observed: A few years ago. Me and my wife were going ginseng hunting back in the woods behind our home. It was starting to get warm out, the sun was up. We started over the hilltop, and the underbrush started to get thicker, but we went on. My wife started looking down in this wash out (ditch), I was going along the top of this wash out (the wash out or ditch mind you was about 12 foot deep and 20 wide and goes all the way down this hill about 300 feet). We were just going along looking. I heard some noises coming from across the ditch 20-30 feet away. I thought it might have been a deer or something. I kept on looking in the way the noise was coming. The noise was trees and brush slapping together. I seen some brush moving around, then it stopped. I was looking trying to see what was making the noises, that's when it came into my view. There was this thing with reddish brown hair all over, at least the parts I seen. I only seen from the chest up. I was only 20-30 feet away from it. I could see its dark eyes, face, everything. It looked like a man to me. My wife was still down in the wash out. I could see her. I watch this thing look down at her then back at me. I had a loaded .22 rifle with me but I could not bring the gun up. It watched us for a few minutes then I got up enough nerve to tell my wife to head back up the hill. We was only there about 20 minutes and she asked why we were leaving so fast? I told her to just get up the hill but go slow. I didn't know if it would come after us If we took off running. I watched as she went up the hill. I was walking backwards trying to see where it was and what it was doing. I seen its chest thru the brush as we headed up the hill, that's when my wife seen it too. She started to run but I got her to stop. We made it home. We have had dogs missing only to find them later tore apart, their insides pulled out. This past deer season (2004) I was back behind my house hunting, I started up the hill across from where me and my wife seen Bigfoot. I had a big rock thrown at me. The rock hit in the top of a big tree. I watched it bounce off a tree and hit the ground. I put up my gun looking thru my scope, I couldn't see anything. It was cold day this day.

Also Noticed: The place stunk. In between a skunk and wet dog.

Conditions: around 9 AM. Sunny.

Investigator Commentary by Tony Gerard: I spoke with both witnesses by phone. Apparently, to the witnesses, this daytime sighting is the most dramatic in a long series of events. The husband had the closest and longest look at the creature, although he could see it only from mid-torso up. He described its build as broad and muscular, three to four feet across the shoulders, and six to seven feet tall. The entire body was covered with long, reddish brown hair. The husband described the head shape as being pointed toward the back. No ears were visible. Hair covered the face like "a man with a beard"; the hair was thinner around the eyes and on the forehead. The eyes were large and dark in color. The mouth was wide, with thick, dark lips. The nose was broad and flat. Overall, the face did not project forward in a muzzle, but was flat like a person or a monkey.

After the couple went up the hill away from the creature, it apparently followed them at a distance. Approximately one week later, at dusk, the wife was in the backyard when "the dogs went crazy barking". She then saw a creature "just standing" in the woods about seventy-five to a hundred feet away. She described this creature as having more blondish brown hair and did not think it was the same animal that her and her husband had seen earlier.

The rock-throwing incident occurred in the same area as the sighting. The husband heard a noise at the top of the ridge and looked up to see a rock "about the size of a football" hit the top of the tree near him and bounce downhill.

"About four years ago", during the summer, the husband was ginseng hunting in the company of his father and brother. They heard what sounded like "Chinamen talking" from one hill to another, then a sound like a tree falling. They then quickly left the area. The wife also related that they found several trees over the years twisted off, "like you'd wring out a washcloth", at a level above a human being's head.

Afterthoughts: I have many reports like this where it seems the Bigfoot seem like they stay in one area for long periods of time. With their size, it seems like it wouldn't necessarily be possible because they require so much food for their body mass. I would speculate that there must be some alternative food source like a dump, habituator, etc. in the area. In many cases it appears most likely that the Bigfoot aren't aggressive, in most cases just moving along.

Year: 2014

Season: Fall
Month: November
State: Georgia
County: Rabun
Nearest Town: Clayton

Observed: I went to a favorite spot for the weekend to get some and quiet and hopefully a monster brown trout. Been going there for years fishing and camping. Not extremely remote but wild and beautiful, nonetheless. It actually an old home place that has long disappeared, nothing remains except the concrete foundation and a narrow-overgrown road that was once the driveway. Was very cold the night before, mid 20's, but the sun was shining bright, and it was starting to warm up. I made the relatively short hike down the old roadbed to my spot by the river. I dropped my pack against a tree and went down the steep embankment to the river's edge to check the water and soak up some sunshine to warm up. After a few minutes I heard what I thought was another fisherman or someone above me where the old foundation was. I thought "great, so much for peace and quiet, must be hardcore trout fisherman like me to be out here in the cold weather". I walked back up the embankment expecting to see people, what I saw in broad daylight, probably 30-40 yards directly in front of me was what I can only describe as what appeared to be a fully erect gorilla, except his face didn't protrude out, it was flatter, and the hair was the color of a squirrel, browns, black, silver, and a slight tint of red when the sun reflected off of him. He was standing there, head slightly tilted back, squinted his eyes, soaking up the sunshine, just as I was. I couldn't comprehend what I was looking at first. My first thought was "what am I looking at?" Second thought was "God, look how big he is". It was incredibly muscular, at least four feet wide at the shoulders, 7-8 feet in height, massive animal. The skin was a darkish gray color around the face, head was extremely pointed, like a dunce hat almost, no neck, large pectorals visible under the hair. Eye color was a shade of amber. It was squinting in the bright sun, soaking up some warmth. He didn't really see me at first, I don't think. I did just kind of pop up over the embankment. I think he knew I was there but didn't really know where. He could have been trying to smell me. I watched this massive, beautiful animal standing there in the sun for 15-20 seconds. I had a feeling of amazement, wonder and actually privilege. I knew that what I was looking at was truly one of Gods immaculate creations. It was beautiful, big, and scary as hell, but beautiful. Hair was clean, looked almost groomed. Very healthy animal. After 15-20 seconds of seeing this, I actually stepped up over the embankment all the way into view and I was said something out loud like "hey big boy, aren't you a pretty thing!" That's when he finally saw me. It dropped its head down and froze. I could tell I surprised it. It wouldn't make eye contact. I could see its whole posture change. It became very shy and acted like that it was hoping that as long as it didn't look at me I wouldn't see it. It was like a bashful child. I took a few steps toward it and said "hey big boy", or something to that effect, and that was enough for him. He turned to his left and he was out of there. I could hear the limbs and leaves rustle as he made his getaway. He moved like a deer going up the mountain, fast, fast. Didn't see him but I could hear him. After probably 5 seconds the rustling stopped and it was totally silent. Then I clearly hear what sounded like someone doing a drum roll of wooden stakes on a wooden table. Three brat-tat-tat-tats, very quick, very clear, definitely not a woodpecker. No doubt in my mind it was him. He had traversed the mountainside and was on the ridgeline above me in no more than 5-10 seconds. Unbelievable. I never felt threatened, never felt afraid. Was a feeling of privilege and respect. I set camp and stayed at that spot for the night and all of the next day but never saw it again. Spent most of my life in those mountains and feeder creeks, backpacking, fishing for brook trout. Thought that I knew all there was to know. That day changed my life. Made me question not only my sanity and eyesight (I'm not crazy and have 20/20 vision, but my understanding of the natural world. I have been back several times but haven't seen him.

Conditions: Full sun.

Investigator Commentary by Dave Bakara: I spoke with the witness by phone, and he was still affected by what he saw in November of 2014. He seemed honest and concise in the retelling of events. This special, out-of-the-way place he fished at was a favorite spot. Though somewhat out of the way, it wasn't completely remote. After arriving at approximately 12:30 p.m., he stood briefly in the morning sun to take in the warmth, as it was chilly the night before. He then walked down a short distance to the river and set up to camp and fish for a couple of days.

After a short time, he began to hear someone up the bank where he had just come from, shifting and rustling, and his thought was, "Oh, great, so much for a quiet day," and he began to walk up to see who it was. As he crested the bank, he was greeted with the sight of a huge hairy, manlike ape. It was standing straight up with its head tilted up to the morning sun. It stood between seven and eight feet tall. Its eyes were squinted, and its long arms hung straight down. It was standing in thick ground clutter, and he could only see from the thighs up. He described it as a clean, groomed animal with the hair color of a fox squirrel, brown with tints of black, brown, red, and silver. He said he could see the hair moving slightly in the morning breeze, and there was no matting or dirt on the creature. Its eyes were amber yellow and brown. It looked "absolutely beautiful". He detected no odor, said the creature had no neck, with the head planted squarely on the shoulders, and had a distinctly pointed head. He also noted it was definitely a robust and super muscular male with huge pectoral muscles (like a muscle gorilla) that flexed as it deeply breathed the mountain air.

He watched the animal for approximately twenty seconds (said it was like twenty minutes), then felt overwhelmed by what he was looking at, and wanted to get a little closer. He stepped over a small log on the trail and took two steps, then quietly said something like, "Well, look at you, you big beautiful thing." This is when the creature went into a completely different mood. He said it instantly went into a position of a busted dog that got into trouble. The witness again spoke gently to it, but it wouldn't look at him, looked only down, then backed up to try to blend into a large tree that stood a few feet behind him. That proved unsuccessful, as he was just too big for the tree. It then turned to its left and retreated into the forest, quickly like a deer, but not actually running. The witness said it covered ground that would have taken him thirty minutes to scale in ten seconds. After it made its way to the other ridge, he heard a rapid tat-a-tat-tat-tat. It sounded like a rapid tree knock, but incredibly fast. He likened it to the speed of a drumroll. The witness stated that this encounter has changed his whole understanding of the natural world.

Afterthoughts: I've pictured many times how I would like a Bigfoot encounter to happen, and surely it would be something like this. Over the year, with the hundreds of witnesses I have interviewed, I have come to the opinion that most of the time a Bigfoot will not move unless it's been spotted. For instance, if a car or hunter is coming, it may squat, resembling a stump, or stand behind a tree even if it's smaller. I've seen videos of world-class whitetail deer do something similar. They were in the field, and when a car came, they lay down and put their horns lower than the grass in the field.

Year: 2019
Season: Fall
Month: October
State: Virginia
County: Roanoke
Nearest Town: Vinton

Observed: It was last year (2019) near the Blue Ridge Parkway. Me and my boyfriend were working for the Roanoke Times delivering newspapers when this encounter happened. We delivered anywhere from 12AM to 6 AM. We were almost done with the route when we went to turn down this dead-end maintenance road since there were houses at the end that got the paper. It was around 3:30-4:00 AM. While my boyfriend was going down the gravel end maintenance road the headlights caught a glimpse of this thing standing right where the grass met the road. It stood about 7 feet tall, and it took off up the hill. It kinda walked fast, not necessarily ran. It was dark brown and had shaggy like fur. It was on 2 feet and walked like a human with its arms swaying right below the knees. I screamed out for my boyfriend to stop the car, but by the time his reaction time kicked in whatever it was had made its way up the hill. My boyfriend positioned the car so the lights would shine up that hill and that's when we saw 2 bright glowing red/yellow eyes looking back at us. What was strange was it was hiding behind a huge tree and how high the eyes were up from the ground, was close to 7 feet high. You could clearly see the eyes blink. We sat there for approximately 10 minutes and finally decided to finish the route and come back. We did eventually come back after we got done with the last house and it was gone, but you could see where tree limbs and grass was pushed down from where it was standing on the side of the road. Maybe less than a month before that we had encounter where we had heard tree knocks while on our route, from deep down in the woods maybe a neighborhood or two over. It scared us so bad that when we heard it, we just bagged up the newspaper and threw it on the side of the road.

Also Noticed: There was a lot of deer while doing our route, but where this encounter happened we never saw a single deer in that area for the 5 months we delivered that area 7 days a week.

Investigator Commentary by Matt Moneymaker: I spoke with Brandi at length. She seems very credible. She and her boyfriend no longer deliver newspapers but still live in the area. They stopped delivering newspapers because they both had day jobs, so they had very little time to sleep in between. It wasn't sustainable. Newspaper delivery drivers work in the wee hours of the morning. They are often witnesses to Sasquatches and other wildlife that no one else gets to see due to the hours they operate. The neighborhood in question is on the edge of Roanoke County. The other side of the county line is Bedford County with a large, densely forested wild area. It is private land containing two large reservoirs. The nearest one is Falling Creek Reservoir. The encounter happened on Falling Creek Drive. The habitat is hilly with a mix of oaks, conifers, and loads of deer.

Afterthoughts: Concerning the lack of deer in the presence of Bigfoot, I have witnesses that know the Bigfoot are in the area when this happens. You may remember that I pay attention to the area and dates when the normal wildlife disappears from my game cameras. The majority of sightings occur from dusk to dawn when less people are active. This would lead us to believe that while Bigfoot may move during the day, they are more active at night.

Year: 1985
Season: Summer
Month: June
State: North Carolina
County: Macon
Nearest Town: Franklin

Observed: Franklin, 1985, Walnut Creek Road area. Walking up an old logging trail to the top of the mountain on border of Nantahala National Forest, I rounded a blind curve and saw a creature squatting possibly taking crawdaddy's out of creek that crossed the logging road. I froze in fear, it stood up and looked at me and I turned around and ran back down the road.

Conditions: 2 PM, Clear.

Investigator Commentary by Jeff Carpenter: I spoke with the witness by phone. He was very sincere, and wanted to recount the sighting he had around June of 1985. The event had a profound impact on him, and it has always stayed with him.

The witness was around twelve years of age at the time of the sighting, and he was on a family trip to their cabin in Western North Carolina. The cabin is located near the Cullasaja Gorge on a very remote mountain. At the time of the sighting, no other homes were near or above the cabin. The area above the cabin was very steep with mountain creeks. The witness stated that the family let the kids play and explore the area, but they had to stay close and wear a whistle.

On this day, he was by himself, and he had gone farther up the mountain on an old logging road. The road had turned very steep up the mountain and then made a 180-degree turn. As he came around the turn, he saw the creature squatted by the creek. At first he didn't know what to think about it, until it stood up and turned its head to him. He stated that he froze in fear for a few seconds and then panicked as he ran down the mountain, blowing his whistle. His family got to him when he got closer to the cabin. They did not believe him and tried to convince him he saw something else. He stated as far as he can recall, no one went up to the site to look for tracks, etc.

He stated that he had seen many wild animals, and he is very sure that what he saw was not a bear at all. The witness was very concrete in what details he remembered. He estimated he was about forty yards away, and the animal had brown matted hair. The height was around seven feet tall, and he recalled it not having any neck at all. It had shoulders with long arms, and he was very sure it was on two feet. He thought it might have been eating something from the creek but didn't recall seeing anything. A pool is located in the creek at this location he stated.

I am very familiar with this location, as it is located near the entrance to the Cullasaja Gorge in Macon County, North Carolina. The area is located on a remote mountain with mountain streams and many rock formations such as cliffs and steep gorges. Deer, turkey, and wild boar are found in this area as well as fish and cray-fish in the many mountain streams.

Afterthoughts: We commonly hear that Bigfoot has no neck. In fact, this is probably one of the most common attributes witnesses relay. All mammals have seven vertebrae except some sloths and mana-tee's so it's clear that Bigfoot does as well. I believe that Bigfoot's trapezius muscles are so developed making it appear as though there is no neck. Notice the Bigfoot possibly after crawdads? Snakes, crawdads, and oodles of other things that are common through Appalachia but not something that comes to mind when we think of food.

Year: 2004
Season: Fall
Month: November
State: Pennsylvania
County: Allegheny

Observed: It was about 4:30 AM and I had just settled into my tree stand for a day of hunting. It was extremely quiet which the first thing that I had noticed. It was going on about 5:00 AM when I hear what sounded like a log being hit with another log. I brushed it off as something was going on at the new construction site at the top of the hill. At about 5:20 AM I heard something walking back and to my left toward the top of the hill that I was sitting on. I was about 1/4 the way up the hill and this was near the top where I heard it. I knew the walking was bipedal and at this point I got very angry about somebody trespassing and ruining my day of deer hunting. As the noise got closer the sun was up just enough I could skyline this huge "man" walking across the top of the ridge. I looked at him through my binos and well it wasn't any man. I know this Bigfoot had to be

7'5" tall and at least 650 pounds. He was dark brown or black in color, unable to tell exactly due to lighting issues. I wasn't able to make out facial features. His hair was maybe 2 inches long and his hands were definitely below knee level. I put my binos down and it must have been then that he noticed something and within 3 strides he disappeared into a grapevine thicket. The entire actual setting lasted maybe 15 seconds.

Conditions: Sunrise. Started with the knocking at about 4:30 AM.

Investigator Commentary by Robert Gorny: I spoke to the witness by phone, and he had some detail to add to the report: The witness saw the figure at a distance of approximately 275-300 yards. There have been other times when hunting in the same area the witness felt as though he was being watched. A neighbor to the witness has described hearing "hyena laughter" on occasion behind her house. The father of the witness was chopping wood one afternoon when a number of rocks were thrown in his direction. He thought it was his son, but his son was not in the area from where the rocks were thrown.

Afterthoughts: This encounter as well as the other things listed took place all within 2 miles of a major metropolitan/industrial area. I've heard from investigators all over the country about how close some of the Bigfoot are staying relative to urban areas and housing. While it provides the opportunity for expanded food resources, it also must be a challenge to get security in these areas. Maybe it all goes back to how little humans are in the woods anymore.

~

Year: 2015
Season: Fall
Month: September
State: Virginia

County: Bedford

Observed: On September 9, 2015, I was driving down 43W outside of Bedford, Virginia at 11:38 PM when I saw to the right of the road, walking away from the road, a Bigfoot with a child. It was next to the mailbox 4472, where there is a gravel poured drive. At first I thought it was a deer, about the same coloring, but as I got closer, I noticed it was not a deer at all, it was much taller, about 6 ft. As I got closer it appeared the mom (I assume that since there was a baby with it) put the baby down and was bending over for rocks? At that time the baby looked right at me and it looked just like the Wukie (? the furry, hairy creature) on Star Wars and it had a brown looking nose. The baby seemed as surprised to see me as I was them. I guess WE look like aliens to them. The baby was about 3 feet, it hit mom at mid-thigh. I painted circles around the footprints I found the next day, 3 prints, about 36" stride. There first print you come to is the best, prints are difficult to produce in the gravel, but the first one is in fine gravel there are two circles around the footprints I found where it appeared. The mom put the baby down. They were headed into the woods and although there are deer around, there was a path worn in that direction. I reported it to the police department and it was basically ignored.

Investigator Commentary by Charles Kimbrough: I spoke to the witness a few days after she filed the report. She was driving west towards Peaks of Otter at 11:38 PM. Her initial thought was that it was just a deer, but a second later she realized it wasn't a deer, but was a Bigfoot. She could very easily see the bottom half of this creature in her headlights but couldn't see the top half very well. The top half was dark because it was taller than the headlight beam. The lower half appeared to have a reddish-brown colored hair that was about 6" long. The hair didn't appear to be thick but had a fine texture to it.

After the animal crossed the road, it stopped just past the edge of the road and squatted down. It did this to put the Bigfoot child down on the ground. This child was about 3 feet tall and mid-thigh on the adult. The adult did not stand back up straight afterwards but stayed stooped over. The witness thought it was prepared to protect its child at all costs. She believed it was picking up a handful of rocks but couldn't be sure because it didn't throw any at the car. As soon as the child's feet touched the ground, it turned and looked at the car's headlights. She saw them from about 15 feet away. The witness did not stop her car.

The next day she had her landscaper go by this location and look around. There were a couple of tracks in the gravel, but they were not detailed. There was a dead deer lying very near to where she saw the Bigfoot. The deer was not there the previous night. The witness is credible. I have had other reports from the area. I also hosted a private BFRO expedition in April just 3 miles away.

Afterthoughts: Sometimes we just catch Bigfoot in a spot we don't expect them. Caroline Curtis, the secretary of the BFRO, jokingly calls them the BUO, Bigfoot of unknown origin. The witnesses like this, who knew absolutely nothing about Bigfoot or that there were even television shows about Bigfoot, are very compelling. As researcher Matt Moneymaker says, "Bigfoot witnesses are geographic, not demographic." They live in an area that Bigfoot also lives.

I remember a couple who was on one of the West Virginia's *Finding Bigfoot* episodes who pulled out of their driveway to see a Bigfoot walking down the two-lane highway at 4:30 a.m. Later they went back and got hair from the fence there.

$\sim$

Year: 2008
Season: Spring
Month: May
State: West Virginia
County: Lincoln

Nearest Town: Danville

Observed: First of all thank you for taking my story. I was born in Clay County, Kentucky and have lived in several states since: Ohio, Indiana, Pennsylvania, Tennessee, and now West Virginia. My story takes place while living on the West Virginia and Kentucky border in 2008. The coal industry is very important part of the economy in that area. Underground mining requires battery operated equipment due to the exhaust of internal combustion engines. I was working for a company that rebuilt the batteries that ran the equipment. These batteries weigh 100 to 150 pounds each. I picked up some batteries for one of the mines in our area and started on the route. I went down past Charleston, West Virginia and started down Route 3, which led me into a very rural area. The road went from black top to gravel and then to dirt. It was about 5:00 PM and being in the spring of the year the day had begun to wane and evening fall. I had my headlights on as I made my way along the dirt road. I was traveling along about 15 miles per hour and was going along a stream that ran along on my left. I rounded a turn and found a low water bridge crossing the stream. A low water bridge is made of some pipe that allows water to flow through them and then concrete is poured along the top to make a roadway. These are always one lane wide and close to the water. Lining up with the bridge I noticed four deer off to the right with some birds and on the left of the bridge was a bear. I have seen many bears down where I work, but only black bears, some three to four hundred pounds. This one however was very shaggy! I thought, how odd, I've never seen a bear in that area and certainly not one that big. It was sitting on its haunches looking down into the water. I had the driver's side window about halfway down as I approached it. As I got closer I thought, "That's not a bear!" When I got to within about 5 yards of it, it stood up and turned to look at me. It must have been at least 8 feet tall and 4 feet wide at the shoulders, and no neck that I could see. I had never been that close to an animal that size in my life. It was a brindle color, brown, black, and gray, all mingled together. Its head was kind of pointed and no hair on its face, it looked almost human. It didn't look angry or threatening, just kind of interested in me being there. The hair, several inches long, hung down on its arms and its hands were almost to its knees. Bears don't have front legs like that, I should know, I've seen enough of them fairly close up and they sure don't have hands! As I drove by, it looked down at me in my pick-up truck and I realized how large it was. I was within 5 feet of it when I passed and going about 5 mph as I passed it. There was no foul smell that I can remember and I have heard that that that seems to come with them. Approaching the end of the bridge I looked in my outside mirror and it turned and stepped off the bridge into what must have been 4 feet of water and it didn't even come to its waist. I remember saying to myself, "That wasn't a bear!" I watched it cross the stream and climb up the opposite bank, with a hand over hand motion, holding onto trees as it went. Coming back that way from my delivery, it was dark, and I saw no sign of it anywhere. Several years have gone by and I am now 71 years old. I had not told anyone about what I saw until recently. I shared the story with my father-in-law and told him I would understand if he didn't believe me, but to my surprise he had worked in that area and said, "There's something down there that people have claimed to see for years." I hope you have enjoyed my story and swear that it's true.

Investigator Commentary by Dr. Russ Jones: In addition I can add: The encounter happened before the town of Foster. The witness was in his fifties at the time and has been in ministry for fifty years. The low-water bridge has six culverts about four feet high. The Bigfoot was sitting down, looking into the water. The witness believes the sound of the water and his slow rate of speed kept the Bigfoot from hearing his approach.

He can picture the Bigfoot and scene like it was yesterday. The Bigfoot, which stood up when he got within fifteen feet, had a black face, black eyes, no muzzle or pointed ears, and no hair on the face. The nose was humanlike but broader and flatter. The head was higher in back but not real pointed. The arms seemed disproportionately long. The Bigfoot looked like a muscular, well-defined athlete; it was an amazing sight to see. He states that, "I've spent a lot of time in the woods, and I know what I saw. I would swear in a court of law."

Afterthoughts: This report, like many I have shared, has never been made public. As soon as I got it, I immediately looked at a map to see if I could figure out why the Bigfoot would be in the area. The reality is that while all of West Virginia is good terrain to host a Bigfoot, this location was not even close to what one would consider unusual. That being said, maybe there is some magical food source at the head of the hollow, who's to say.

I found the witness upright and compelling. Many of the reports that I have, the witness won't even allow me to share, so they certainly didn't claim their sighting for attention, fame, or money. Many, like this witness, didn't share the story for a long time. His father-in-law claims that almost monthly miners were seeing something in that area that they couldn't identify. Much of the land along this road is now private property, but of course, like much of Appalachia, there are many miles in between roads and always steep mountainsides.

I hosted the *Finding Bigfoot* television show last summer for their special episode, and it's fairly close cross-country to where they shot the film.

AFTERWORD

Here we are at the end of the Appalachian Bigfoot book. It's been seven years since I wrote *Tracking the Stone Man*, and it's fun to think about what has changed in that time frame. It's hard to believe how quickly time passes. Some say that it goes quicker as we age; scientists speculate that's because we don't really learn as many new things as when we are young. You know, kind of older "already seen everything", so in turn time passes quicker. I'm hoping that we learn a lot of new things about Bigfoot in the next seven years.

In terms of evidence in the field, we are now able to analyze the footprints more scientifically and with some new visualization techniques. It's being shown and reinforced by footprint casts that proposed Bigfoot tracks represent different structural and functional traits compared to other primates, including human anatomy. Even if one naively believes all footprints to be fake, which is a big reach, many of the prints show dynamic motion consistent with a living creature.

Frankly, the Bigfoot researchers who specialize in foot anatomy, think Dr. Jeff Meldrum, know more than traditional scientists regarding this anatomy. Sadly, as a result, the scientists just don't know enough or don't have the interest in actually learning enough to give an educated opinion. I talk about it on podcasts all the time. People are so busy with their lives, relationships, work, kids, etc. that unless you have a vested interest in Bigfoot, it just doesn't enter into your thinking much. Now that doesn't mean that people don't have opinions even though they don't spend time in isolated woodlands or keep up with what is going on in Bigfoot research. Many people who think they are very interested or "into" Bigfoot are surprised that I invest about twenty hours or more a week; it's at that point they recognize that maybe they aren't into Bigfoot that much.

The thermal camera is evolving. While there are cheap options like the smart phone attachments and the Flir Scout, the reality is that it still costs around $4,000 to get a good thermal. Flir has some competition in the market, namely Pulsar. The Pulsar Helion 2 XP50 is a quality unit for a serious researcher. They have the Pro unit coming out soon. The BFRO has their own small handheld unit, which is popular. I know Matt Moneymaker has some innovative ideas coming out with thermal devices in the future. There have been quite a few quality thermal Bigfoot videos come out in the past seven years, including a great one from the BFRO in California. The thermals are also being mounted on drones. Unfortunately the scientific community isn't interested in much thermal footage.

Who would have thought that drones would have been as popular as they are now, even with licenses and classes? Matt Moneymaker has really been interested in thermal units on drones and believes they could have a bright future in the field. I think comprehensively with game camera footage, witness testimony, and track casts, all in the same area, we could have something that the public would find compelling. Maybe not the scientists, but of course, it's largely going to take a body or body part, as you know I believe.

Sony has a camera called the A7 that will make dark almost light for taking traditional pictures. Doug Hajicek, of the television show *MonsterQuest*, has been pairing the A7 with a 400mm zoom cannon lens. If you think you can get close enough to get a Bigfoot in the clear, it may be a good option. I love getting to listen and talk to Doug, as he always has innovative ideas. All of these things are very expensive and have drawbacks. Thermals can't see through leaf cover or brush and is used at night largely. Cameras like the A7 require a clear shot. For the money, game cameras with creative setups are probably the cheapest way for a good shot.

If knowledge is power, there has never been more easy access to Bigfoot information. Bigfoot podcasts are available by the thousands. I personally listen to them all the time. Some witnesses are suspect and/or hard to listen to, but some are exceptional, and in the course of time, it's possible to pick up recurring Bigfoot behavior traits.

Woo, the paranormal aspect, has continued to proliferate. As people's knowledge of the outdoors and time in the outdoors continue to decrease, I suspect it will continue to spread. Allowing for the physical and intellectual laziness that it attracts and proliferates. I can remember ten to fifteen years ago it was rare that anyone was involved with paranormal considerations involving Bigfoot. Investigator and author Thom Powell was one of the few who messed with it at all. No one would question Thom's sincerity and intelligence, and I long for those days.

The interest in Bigfoot has continued, and there are more conferences than ever, largely well attended. COVID didn't stop Bigfoot interest. The television show *Finding Bigfoot* can still attract a large audience even after being off the air for two years and being hidden on Discovery Plus for its special episode.

What have I learned in the last seven years? Well, I have quit ambulance chasing every report and have zeroed in on a few areas as opposed to being anywhere within a six-hour range of being home. Previously I had found that I was coming across Bigfoot-type evidence roughly every two hundred hours, and now I am at about half the time. Using my "Bigfoot Action" calendar, I am having much more success and believe I had my first, albeit brief, sighting. Game cameras have kind of been known as my "thing", and I think I am getting closer to getting a good pic. For sure, I am doing a better job at understanding the animals in my areas and their patterns and what that may mean in terms of Bigfoot.

I would be remiss without speculating what the next seven years may bring. I expect there to be a new type and improvement in testing DNA. Hopefully this will make the testing cheaper and more accessible for Bigfoot researchers. I expect to see many more improved images with thermal imagery, mostly because of drones. I expect to see a greater interest in Bigfoot by some scientists. It's my understanding that some of the younger academics are more open-minded than their stodgy predecessors. Half of the Bigfoot researchers will try to innovate and change, and half will be attracted to woo pathways and terminology.

For me personally? In all likelihood I will be retired, affording me even more time in the field. It's hard to believe that here in 2021, I will have been in practice thirty years. I plan to probably live full time at my farm in Ohio, where I will rigorously try to habituate. I will move almost all my research to two areas, which should allow for my success to improve even more. This past year I have turned down all speaking engagements except two. I am concentrating on spending more time in the field, and giving up eight to ten weekends a year to speak won't allow that. I feel a sense of urgency in Bigfoot research.

What will these next seven years bring for you? Will you sit on the sidelines or decide to find a location that you can get to each week or two and spend some time hiking with your eyes and ears open? Bigfoot research is one of the few chances left that citizen scientists can make a difference in something that if proven may prove to be the biggest discovery in modern history. I would be remiss if after over two hundred thousand patient visits, I didn't remind you that being out in the woods is good for your health, both physical and mental. Our lives in this time are so loud that it's hard to hear ourselves think. Take that chance and get out where you can hear, and maybe, just maybe, you will hear something that sounds like wood hitting a tree.

APPENDIX 1:

INVESTIGATOR QUESTIONNAIRE

Investigator Questionnaire: I thought it might be interesting and fun to have some noted Bigfoot Researchers answer several questions. The researchers take cases in Appalachia and have all been doing so for at least several years. While many researchers have their own independent beliefs, which have been developed through research and experience, it's important to note that many have come by different paths. It's important that researchers spend time together to further understanding of the Bigfoot phenomenon.

Matt Pruitt has been researching the Sasquatch phenomenon since 2002, and subsequently began conducting field research in 2004. His pursuit of the phenomenon has led him across the entire continent, primarily focusing on the Southern Appalachians, the Pacific Northwest, and the US Interior Highlands. Though he hasn't had a visual observation of a Sasquatch, he has had experiences over the years that were consistent with the phenomenon as described by testimonial claims of Sasquatch witnesses. At the present time Matt is still diligently testing the hypothesis that an as-yet-unrecognized species of a nonhuman ape occurs in specific portions of North America.

In addition to his fieldwork, Matt engages in numerous public-facing discussions about the subject in various media and at speaking events. Matt is on the board of directors of the North American Wood Ape conservancy (NAWAC), and is the co-host and co-producer of their official podcast *Apes Among Us*. He is also the producer and editor of the popular podcast *Bigfoot and Beyond with Cliff and Bobo*.

Matt is not only one of the nicest guys in the field, but whenever you hear him talk, he makes you thankful that he is in the field. He makes all of us look brighter by his inclusion. I can't help but feel that if we had a "group" of Matt Pruitts, the mystery might be solved much quicker.

What age and experience got you interested in Bigfoot?

I had an experience with four other friends in the summer of 1999 when I was seventeen years old. We had been aggregating stories from older people in the community related to strange or "haunted" places, many of which described experiences that occurred on a particular mountain. One of the more compelling stories that we received involved two men who were staying in an abandoned cabin located somewhere on the mountain. As such, the five of us went out to camp at the foot of the mountain, planning to hike up an over-grown logging road at night to locate the cabin. One of my companions brought along a VHS-C camcorder to document any strange activity that we might encounter.

During the hike, we distinctly heard at least two "things" stalking us in the dense forest. These unseen interlopers proceeded to break large branches, striking them loudly against trees. In addition to these percussive sounds, we heard a number of vocalizations and a large tree being broken and crashing to the ground in close proximity to us. The sounds were intimidating enough that we eventually aborted the hike, ran back to our vehicles, and drove back to my mother's house.

We reviewed the video that my friend had captured and were able to hear the vocalizations, branch breaking, and percussive sounds clearly. We returned the next morning to retrieve our tent and make the hike up the mountain in the daylight. We were able to locate the remains of the abandoned cabin, but saw no clear sign of the things we'd encountered the previous night. Over the next two years, we made subsequent visits to the mountain and repeated the night hike, but never experienced anything like what we had heard on that initial encounter.

Around 2002, I stumbled across information related to the Sasquatch phenomenon online. At first, the concept seemed ridiculous to me, but as I read through many of the testimonies related to Sasquatch behaviors and intimidation displays, I was struck by how similar the accounts were to our own experience. Moreover, the vocalization and "wood knock" recordings available online that were attributed to the Sasquatches were remarkably consistent with the sound that we'd heard and recorded. I began to explore the possibility that what we'd encountered were animals fitting the description of the apes described by the Sasquatch witnesses, and continue to explore that possibility to this day.

Have you seen a Sasquatch?

Unfortunately, I have not yet seen a Sasquatch. I am diligently trying though!

How long until you believe there is irrefutable proof of Bigfoot, and how do you think it will come to pass?

The official discovery of Sasquatch could happen at any moment. In my estimation, the most likely scenario would be that a Sasquatch is shot and collected by a property owner or homeowner experiencing repeated activity. These sorts of scenarios are reportedly occurring with enough frequency that it's seemingly only a matter of time until a person acting in a defensive capacity takes the opportunity to collect one.

What do you find to be the most compelling evidence of Bigfoot's existence?

In terms of physical evidence, I'm compelled by the documented footprints and impressions. I'm also very compelled by the canon of reliable and credible eyewitness testimonies related to purported observations and encounters.

If time and money were no issue to resolve the Bigfoot enigma, what would you do?

My first instinct would be to facilitate the full-time occupation of the study site of the North American Wood Ape Conservancy (NAWAC) by our experienced members until a specimen is collected. Beyond that approach, I would obtain a large tract of land in suitable habitat and try to replicate the conditions that appear to occur in repeat-visit scenarios. It should be possible to document Sasquatches under those conditions with the requisite equipment, resources, and expertise.

If you could research anywhere, where would you go?

I would be compelled to spend time in the most remote areas that constitute viable habitat, particularly in places where humans almost never venture. There are many places in British Columbia, Alberta, and the Yukon that meet those criteria.

How much time do you spend in the woods each month?

I'm usually in the field at least one long weekend each month—four days and three nights or so. During the summer months, I spend two weeks in the field with the NAWAC.

What frustrates you the most about Bigfoot research?

The most frustrating things that I encounter regularly among proponents would be the proliferation and championing of outlandish claims, the supernatural interpretation of mundane natural occurrences, and the unwillingness to develop familiarity with relevant information. There's a large subset of the Sasquatch proponent community that has abdicated any semblance of a commitment to responsible research and data collection and has instead attempted to construct their own tenuous iterations of what evidence might constitute "proof".

Familiarity with the best evidence and most rigorous analyses of that evidence is paramount, as it establishes qualitative distinctions between pieces of the evidence. Obviously, some pieces of evidence are better than others as pertains to their indication that there might be a biological origin for the Sasquatch phenomenon. When proponents do away with those qualitative distinctions and offer up anything that they encounter as "evidence", then it eradicates a standard of evidence that should be adhered to. Under those conditions, every broken twig, every divot in the ground, and every bump in the night can be proffered as "Sasquatch evidence", which ultimately undermines the validity of the pursuit of Sasquatch altogether. If there are no categorical delineations between the quality of physical elements or claims offered as evidence for the Sasquatch, then all of the evidence and claims become essentially worthless.

It's also been the case that the institutions who do hold a high standard regarding what constitutes evidence are met with scorn by proponents offering substandard data to them in search of validation. This is a complete failure on the part of most proponents to accept the requisite standards that these institutions abide by. This condition has contributed greatly to keeping this subject in the dark. All researchers and proponents need to adhere to the standards of the scientific and academic institutions that they so desperately want to be validated by. The overzealous proponents who create and occupy their own value structures are doing great disservice to the subject and, moreover, to themselves. They're degrading and eroding the serious consideration of the potential reality of the Sasquatch phenomenon.

Do you think that Bigfoot television shows have affected Bigfoot research?

Everything has a cost and a benefit, and the level of interest generated by Sasquatch-related television shows is no different. The overall benefit has been that successful Sasquatch-related series have permitted many reliable investigators and witnesses alike to have a more open dialogue about the phenomenon. These shows have demonstrated that there is an interest among the general public for a resolution to this mystery.

The cost has been the oversensationalized representation of the phenomenon. This creates an incentive for more outlandish claims and has compounded the cost of driving credible witnesses and researchers further from the public discourse. While the proverbial signal indicating the potential existence of these apes has increased, the noise obscuring that signal increases exponentially along with it, driven by the sensational productions and often outright fabrications in an effort to increase the viewership of certain shows.

What do you think of the woo or paranormal aspect of Bigfoot?

I'm currently working on a book project that will address much of this element of the Sasquatch phenomenon. I'm convinced that, if Sasquatches do exist, they're perfectly normal animals that conform to biological and ecological norms. The hypothesis that attempts to explain the Sasquatch phenomenon as being biological is sufficient; there's no need to invoke the metaphysical or supernatural in order to accommodate the reality of the creatures described by this phenomenon.

The paranormal interpretations of the phenomenon are to be expected. Humans have a mystical interpretive schema that's been well established in our species across time and geography, as demonstrated by cultures the world over. As such, if the Sasquatch does exist as a biological species, then we should expect such interpretation to occur. The onus is on us to differentiate between phenomenological experiences and interpretations of these animals, and the objective realities that are being observed. We've already made these distinctions between the mythical representations of known animals and our modern understanding of them but haven't achieved the same degree of differentiation with the Sasquatch yet. The Sasquatch remains unrecognized, and as long as it remains in that liminal space, we should expect the metaphysical claim and interpretations to proliferate.

What do you think of habituation?

I'm not certain that it's possible to habituate Sasquatches in the same manner as other animals can be habituated to human presence or influence. Perhaps the time will come when diligent researchers can demonstrate otherwise, but that's yet to be determined.

What word best describes bigfooting?

Frustrating.

What is something that you believe about Bigfoot that would surprise other people?

I'm not sure whether it would surprise Sasquatch proponents, but I am convinced that the most crucial element of their lifestyle and behavioral repertoire are their cooperative ambush hunting behaviors. This element, when taken into context, does a great deal to explain the Sasquatch phenomenon. One need only study the literature related to other ambush predators to see the consistencies and implications.

What do you think Bigfoot may be?

I think the Asian ape clade that produced *Indopithecus* and *Gigantopithecus* is the most parsimonious ancestral lineage for Sasquatches that we're currently aware of. Of course, the fossil record is incomplete, and there may be an ancestral form that we haven't discovered yet that could serve as a more parsimonious solution. A given clade will produce a radiation of genera, and a given genus will produce a radiation of species. Currently, this sister clade to the orangutan is only represented by two genera: *Indopithecus* and *Gigantopithecus* (previously thought to represent the same genus). Within those two genera, only one species each is represented at present: *I. giganteus* and *G. blacki*. It isn't at all likely that these were the only two genera produced by this clade, and it's not at all likely that each genus only produced a single respective species. As such, we can responsibly assume that this Asian ape line took many forms over the large temporal and geographic spans that we're currently aware of, and that they likely extended in both time and area. That, coupled with their access to North America via Beringia, makes this lineage the most likely known candidate in my estimation.

Dusty Ruth was employed as a state investigator for twenty-five years and then an executive for a federal agency for another fifteen years. He is a trained interviewer and interrogator. He has been interested in Bigfoot for fifty years. He has led Bigfoot expeditions in several states. He has spoken in public and at conferences concerning Bigfoot. He lives in Ohio. Dusty is one of those guys you would be hard-pressed to find someone who dislikes him. On the expeditions he leads, many times the first-timers (newbies) are nervous but instantly feel comfortable and welcome with Dusty.

Have you seen a Bigfoot?

I believe I have seen a Bigfoot three times, and each was with a thermal camera, twice in Kentucky and once in Ohio.

How long until you think there is irrefutable proof of Bigfoot?

I don't know if there will ever be enough evidence to convince everyone to accept it as irrefutable proof. I believe for it to come to pass, the government will have to acknowledge it, or a very important person in a position of power will have to find and produce a body. I am not an advocate of killing one, I mean one that has died naturally or been struck by a vehicle.

What do you find is the most compelling piece of Bigfoot evidence?

I think the most compelling evidence is the Patterson-Gimlin film.

If time and money weren't an issue, what would you due to prove Bigfoot's existence?

To be honest, I don't research to prove their existence to anyone. I do research to learn as much as I can about them and then to share that knowledge with others who wish to hear it. I won't waste my time arguing with anyone over their existence. If time and money were not an issue, I would be interested in radio telemetry in tracking them.

Bucket list, if you could go one place to research, where would it be?

Ohio, where I live. There are plenty of them here, and I prefer to study the behavioral and physical characteristics of the local ones first.

How much time a month would you guess that you spend in the woods?

I'd estimate I spend about fifty-two to fifty-six hours a month in the woods.

What frustrates you the most about Bigfoot research?

What frustrates me the most about Bigfoot research is that I didn't become more involved when I was young.

Do you think Bigfoot television shows have affected Bigfoot research?

I think some shows have been good for Bigfoot research by increasing the interest, but I don't like some of the silly things that the characters are made to do for entertainment purposes. I also don't like when the shows embellish the truth or lie about where an encounter happened.

What do you think of the woo or paranormal aspect of Bigfoot?

At this time, I believe Bigfoot is flesh and blood, but I try to keep an open mind. Just because I didn't experience something doesn't mean that someone else didn't. I will admit that some claims have been difficult to accept.

What do you think of Bigfoot habituation?

I think the person doing it had better be fully aware of the possible consequences of their actions, especially if they leave food for them. There have been many reports of those actions having a bad outcome.

What word best describes Bigfoot?
I would say mysterious or amazing describes Bigfoot the best.

What is something you believe about Bigfoot that would surprise most people?
Ha! For some people I know, just the fact that I believe Bigfoot exists and that I spend so much time studying them would surprise them.

Dr. Kenny Brown. Dr. Brown is a family doctor in Southern Ohio. He is an outdoorsman with an expertise in edibles. He has been specializing in long-duration recordings for years. He is truly the next generation of Bigfooters, bright, engaged, and in the woods when not in with a patient. He has a smile for everyone and is humble with his great knowledge of the outdoors. He is the type of person who makes you feel safe when you are in the woods with him. If because of him irrefutable proof was gained, I would not be surprised at all that it was he who produced it. Everyone likes him and his wonderful family of researchers affectionately known as the "Brown family".

Have you seen a Bigfoot?
I cannot say for sure if I have ever seen a Sasquatch. One afternoon I was driving home on a busy highway and had something appear from the side of the highway that looked to be running next to a guardrail, then going back down the same hill. I caught a very brief glimpse of it, probably one whole second, but I distinctly remember my jaw dropping from seeing what looked like something on two legs running with muscular legs. It was lighter color, almost light gray, and I remember wondering what in the world I had just seen. My dashcam was recording the whole time, and I estimate it was about seventy meters away. I still have to do a recreation, but the creature

appeared right after a full-size semi had just passed where it had appeared, and it ran close to a big yellow sign on the same side of the road.

How long until you believe there is irrefutable proof of Bigfoot, and how do you think it will come to pass?

I think the most likely way there could be irrefutable proof of Sasquatches is if one is killed and brought in, whether a full-body specimen from a hunter or a large enough piece of tissue from being hit by a car. I do, however, believe that consistent reproducible video footage obtained from a location capable of having a Sasquatch approach close in some way, e.g., baiting, could potentially convince a great audience to allow for more funding from academia to pursue this subject more closely.

What do you find to be the most compelling piece of Bigfoot evidence?

I think the 1967 Patterson-Gimlin film is hands down the best piece of evidence to date for the existence of Sasquatch. From someone who has closely studied human anatomy via cadavers and exercise science, there is clear visualization of musculature in motion and a unique gait pattern, and in my opinion a potential suit could not feasibly be made at that point in time in 1967 to accurately represent what is observed in this film.

If time and money weren't an issue, what would you do to prove Bigfoot's existence?

I think the best place to start in this case is to employ better, more reliable methods of capturing footage. Examples would include better thermal imagers with aerial devices to capture footage up close. If successful, I believe this would attract more scientific interest and hopefully effort to look at the subject more seriously.

Bucket list: if you could just go one place to research, where would it be?

In Ohio! If it had to be a different state, I would spend more time in South Dakota, as that was where my first experience was.

How much time would you guess that you spend in the woods each month?

On a regular work/life schedule, I'm guessing I spend an average of twenty-five hours a week, so about a hundred hours a month, in the woods.

What frustrates you about Bigfoot research?

The politics in this subject is what frustrates me the most. If everyone could respect one another's work and/or join together to share more ideas and research, this topic would be much further than it is now.

Do you think the Bigfoot television shows have affected Bigfoot research?

I think the Bigfoot television shows have definitely brought a larger crowd to this subject, which I think is a good thing in many ways to draw attention to this field to allow for production of more evidence. However, there are also a fair share of negatives that come with this.

What do you think of the woo or paranormal aspect of Bigfoot?

My personal belief is that Sasquatches are a flesh and blood creature, whether ape or hominid. While I keep an open mind, there isn't any consistent, reliable evidence in my eyes for the paranormal/woo aspect of Sasquatch to be true; like how there are footprint casts of Sasquatches.

What do you think of habituation?

I think there have been prior instances where Sasquatches have been observed at a location on multiple different occasions from something to entice them closer. If done successfully, I believe this could be a method to obtain great evidence, but the unfortunate aspect of this is the unpredictability.

What word best describes Bigfoot?
Rare.

What is something that you believe about Bigfoot that would surprise most people?
I believe it's possible Sasquatches are capable of infrasound. We have come to know that tigers, elephants, and other animals can produce infrasound for various needs, including for hunting and communicating, so it's entirely possible that they are capable of producing infrasound.

APPENDIX 2:

BIGFOOT NAMES IN APPALACHIA

Bigfoot names historically in Appalachia—listed after dash if for a general specific area.

- Yahoo
- Grassman—Ohio
- Hairy Savage—Cherokee Indians
- Stone Giant—Iroquois Indians
- Stone Man—Cherokee Indians
- Stone Coat—Seneca Indians
- Hairy Man
- Wild Man
- Devil Monkey
- Tall Man—Creek Indians

APPENDIX 3:

BEST BIGFOOT COUNTIES IN APPALACHIA

Most popular counties for a Bigfoot sighting in each state of Appalachia. Keep in mind that many states only have parts of their states in Appalachia, and we are only including those counties.

- Alabama: Morgan, Walker
- Georgia: White, Walker
- Kentucky: Lawrence, Pike
- Maryland: Montgomery, Washington
- Mississippi: Tishomingo, Marshall
- New York: Cattaraugus, Steuben
- North Carolina: Swain, Macon
- Ohio: Guernsey, Columbiana
- Pennsylvania: Allegheny, Clearfield
- South Carolina: Oconee, Spartanburg
- Tennessee: Sevier, Wilson
- Virginia: Giles, Bland
- West Virginia: Pendleton, Randolph

In terms of the states with the most overall sightings, Ohio is number one, and it's not really close. Kentucky would be number two in

Appalachia, but many of the states are very similar and close. Remember that states like Kentucky have my friend Charlie Raymond, who is very active, so report numbers are higher. Ohio has a ton of researchers, so that drives its numbers higher. Also consider a place like Randolph County, West Virginia. It's one of the least populated counties per square mile in the whole Eastern United States, yet has a number of sightings rivaling most counties anywhere in Appalachia. This tells me that they must have a healthy Bigfoot population.

Of course, this is a good starting point when trying to find your own spot to go. Skip the well-known places like Salt Fork in Ohio, as there's a lot of people around yelling and hitting trees. Investigators in general will be skeptical of evidence you may pull from places like that. Go for smaller and isolated state parks or refuges that are in good counties and states. Remember that the only animal that goes somewhere without a reason is a human. Try to figure out the significance of the good locations. What do they have that other locations do not? More importantly, of course, is finding something close to you that you can get to and learn about.

ABOUT THE AUTHOR

Dr. Russ Jones has been in private practice for over 30 years and consumed with the Bigfoot mystery for longer than that. *"The Appalachian Bigfoot"*, is his second book, the first being the award winning *"Tracking the Stone Man"*.

After attending Huntington College on a baseball scholarship, he graduated from Palmer College of Chiropractic. He has a BS degree and Doctor degrees.

Dr. Jones is also a Certified Master Naturalist. He attempts to mix a science background with a lifetime of hunting and trapping knowledge to gather possible evidence of an undiscovered North American primate.

He enters the woods with his faithful black lab "Shade" to tend his dozens of professional game cameras and look for tracks year round in Appalachia.

Made in the USA
Las Vegas, NV
05 December 2022

60995751R00135